Radical Hospitality

Series Board

James Bernauer

Drucilla Cornell

Thomas R. Flynn

Kevin Hart

Richard Kearney

Jean-Luc Marion

Adriaan Peperzak

Thomas Sheehan

Hent de Vries

Merold Westphal

Michael Zimmerman

John D. Caputo, *series editor*

PERSPECTIVES IN
CONTINENTAL
PHILOSOPHY

RICHARD KEARNEY
AND MELISSA FITZPATRICK

Radical Hospitality
From Thought to Action

FORDHAM UNIVERSITY PRESS
New York ■ 2021

Copyright © 2021 Fordham University Press

All rights reserved. No part of this publication may be reproduced, stored in a retrieval system, or transmitted in any form or by any means—electronic, mechanical, photocopy, recording, or any other—except for brief quotations in printed reviews, without the prior permission of the publisher.

Fordham University Press has no responsibility for the persistence or accuracy of URLs for external or third-party Internet websites referred to in this publication and does not guarantee that any content on such websites is, or will remain, accurate or appropriate. Fordham University Press also publishes its books in a variety of electronic formats. Some content that appears in print may not be available in electronic books.

Fordham University Press also publishes its books in a variety of electronic formats. Some content that appears in print may not be available in electronic books.

Visit us online at www.fordhampress.com.

Library of Congress Cataloging-in-Publication Data available online at https://catalog.loc.gov.

Printed in the United States of America

23 22 21   5 4 3 2 1

First edition

*For Jimmy Mahoney,
Guestbook pioneer and friend*

Contents

Introduction. Why Hospitality Now? — *1*

PART I: FOUR FACES OF HOSPITALITY: LINGUISTIC, NARRATIVE, CONFESSIONAL, CARNAL
Richard Kearney

1. Linguistic Hospitality: The Risk of Translation — *17*
2. Narrative Hospitality: Three Pedagogical Experiments — *24*
3. Confessional Hospitality: Translating across Faith Cultures — *43*
4. Carnal Hospitality: Gesturing beyond Apartheid — *49*

PART II: HOSPITALITY AND MORAL PSYCHOLOGY: EXPLORING THE BORDER BETWEEN THEORY AND PRACTICE
Melissa Fitzpatrick

5. Hospitality beyond Borders: The Case of Kant — *61*
6. Impossible Hospitality: From Levinas to Arendt — *75*
7. Teleological Hospitality: The Case of Contemporary Virtue Ethics — *88*
8. Hospitality in the Classroom — *97*

Postscript. Hospitality's New Frontier: The Nonhuman Other	105
Acknowledgments	*111*
Notes	*113*
Bibliography	*137*
Index	*145*

Radical Hospitality

Introduction
Why Hospitality Now?

This volume addresses a timely challenge for contemporary philosophy: the ethical responsibility of opening borders, psychic and physical, to the stranger. Drawing on key critical debates on the question of hospitality ranging from phenomenology, hermeneutics, and deconstruction to neo-Kantian moral critique and Anglo-American virtue ethics, the book engages with urgent moral conversations regarding the role of identity, nationality, immigration, commemoration, and justice. It also explores novel options for the application of an ethics of hospitality to our current world of border anxiety, boundary disputes, refugee crisis, and, perhaps most pressingly—in light of the 2019 United Nations Intergovernmental Panel on Climate Change report—the looming ecological challenge. We discuss such critical applications in terms not only of our social and political worlds of practice but also within the crucially formative life of the classroom. The move we propose from text to action is ultimately one of pedagogy and praxis.

The climate emergency has turned the relationship between host and stranger into a crisis we confront daily: not only the fundamental task of hosting the environmental stranger—where nature demands to be our guest—but also our response to strangers at our borders. Just think of the border disputes we read about in the daily news: Syria and Turkey, the United States and Mexico, Russia and the Ukraine, Israel and Palestine, North Korea and South Korea, or Northern Ireland and the Republic of Ireland (a perennial dispute made topical again with the Brexit crisis facing Europe as we write). A key controversy in every major election campaign of our time—in the United States, United Kingdom, continental Europe, Asia, and Africa—is that of strangers at the frontier, whether they go by the name of migrant, immigrant, refugee, alien, or invader. Who is in and who is out? Who belongs to the nation and who does not? Who deserves shelter and who does not? Who should stay and who should go? Back to where they came from—if there is anything left for them? Who decides the answer to these questions? And according to what criteria, interests, and intentions?

Thomas Meaney's controversial essay, "Who's Your Dance Partner?" (2019), highlights this question in relation to current EU debates on immigration.[1] Meaney argues that while European politicians try to parse the difference between asylum worthies, economic migrants, and climate refugees and all the while collaborate with the authoritarian regimes that produce them, a wiser approach might be to embrace a different paradox: namely, to heed Kant's cosmopolitan claim that the earth belongs to everyone, and at the same time lessen the dire need for Africans and Asians to come to Europe while insuring that their journey is safer and easier. But rather than think creatively about such possibilities of mutual collaboration, Europe and the UK seem to have settled on "a narrow strip of ground." One proposed name for the next top official of UK Migration is "President for Protecting Our Way of Life," and the EU commissioner speaks of the need for a "Europe That Defends and Protects"—referring, of course, to the protection of existing members of the European Community, not to migrants who seek refuge there. UK Prime Minister Boris Johnson was even less equivocal about immigrants in his defense of a little England for Little Englanders. And the America that Trump wished to make "great again" was one that excluded what he called Mexican "rapists and murders" and Africans from "shithole countries." The crisis is acute, and it is set to worsen exponentially as the climate situation grows more alarming and despotic leaders on every continent increasingly endanger their own peoples. Never has the stranger been more in need of hosts to provide shelter, sustenance, and dignity. And never have the doors of welcome seemed more shut.

Hospitality is a notion as old as human culture. It has been claimed that "civilization begins with the handshake."[2] One needs but a cursory glance at the foundational texts of great mythologies and wisdom traditions to be reminded of this. To mention some classic examples from Western culture: think of the biblical stories of Abraham and Sarah hosting the strangers under the Mamre Tree,[3] of Jesus hosting the strangers on the road to Emmaus (the ministry of Christ began with a marriage feast at Cana and ended with a last supper in Jerusalem).[4] Or think of the ancient Greek epics of Homer (Simone Weil notes this formative ethics of hospitality in her brilliant commentary on the *Iliad*), or the hosting of Hermes and Zeus by Baucis and Philemon in Ovid. The subsequent course of Western literature is full of scenes of hospitality from the feasts of Chaucer and Rabelais to the sharing of food in the classic scenes of Monseigneur Muriel with Jean Valjean in *Les misérables* and the miraculous banquet of *Babette's Feast*. But while our religions, myths and literatures are replete with narratives of hosting and guesting, our history of Western thought has been strangely mute on the topic, at least until recently. If it is true, as Paul Ricoeur says, that "the symbol gives rise to thought," it is high time that "thought" stepped up to the plate. A new hermeneutics of hospitality is needed in our age of mounting hostility. And the need is both epistemological (what can we know?) and ethical (what can we do?).

Contemporary Conversations on Hospitality

Hospitality is a term often heard in today's world but seldom addressed in the Western history of philosophy. While implicit in Levinas's discussion of host and hostage and the overcoming of war in *Totality and Infinity* (1961), or again in some of Ricoeur's later thoughts in *On Translation* (2003), the concept of hospitality per se never received a full philosophical treatment by these or other continental thinkers.[5] In fact, the first real attempt to engage the subject philosophically in a single volume was, arguably, Jacques Derrida's reflection on the subject, *Of Hospitality* (1997), a short essay that was less a sustained systematic argument than a summary transcription of two lectures delivered at L'École des Hautes Études in Paris in 1996. Derrida's sortie into the subject—ranging liberally from Oedipus Rex to our postmodern cyber world—takes the form of an experimental commentary with his seminar interlocutor, Anne Dufourmantelle, and is marked by Derrida's quintessentially quizzical style. It reads as fragmentary exchanges rather than a sustained analysis of the subject. And while Julia Kristeva's *Strangers to Ourselves* (1988) offers rich psychoanalytic and literary resources for an understanding of the stranger, she rarely raises the question of hospitality head on. There is much about strangers as guests but little about the hosts needed to welcome them in the first place, especially in today's inhospitable environment. And there is almost nothing on what it really means to be a host *in practice*.

But in addition to addressing the contemporary philosophy of hospitality in its own right, we also consider it important to frame our analysis in the context of recent discussions of related interest—namely (1) the phenomenology of the gift; (2) the theology of sacred economy; and (3) the postapocalyptic culture of welcome.

Phenomenology of the Gift

First, a word on phenomenological debates on the gift conducted between Jacques Derrida (*The Gift of Death* and *Given Time*), Jean-Luc Marion (*Being Given*), John Caputo (*God, The Gift and Postmodernism*), and Marcel Hénaff (*The Philosophers' Gift: Reexamining Reciprocity*). Departing from the classic anthropologies of gift-giving, promoted by Bronislaw Malinowski and Marcel Mauss (*The Gift*) in the early twentieth century,[6] these contemporary thinkers of the gift point in a new direction: away from socioeconomic ceremonies of reciprocity and toward a gesture of rupture and disinterestedness.

To this effect, Derrida proposes the gift as an impossible gesture without giver or addressee, a suspension of all economies of exchange in favor of absolute and unconditional gratuity. "For there to be a gift, there must be no reciprocity" (*Given Time*).[7] Derrida approaches the subject of gift and givenness through multiple tropes, quotes, and anecdotes without ever actually articulating a coherent conceptual conclusion. (He would doubtless claim this befits the *aporetic* nature of the gift.) Caputo develops the deconstruction of the gift, with welcome clarity, in the direction of a "radical hermeneutics" surpassing all estimations of credit and debit and repudiating the standard theodicy of sacrificial atonement which traditionally accompanied it (where a Savior pays off the ransom of original and accumulated sin). In similar wise, Marion proffers a phenomenology of the gift as a "saturated phenomenon" where the subject's intentionality is overturned by an overwhelming intuition, rendering the receiving subject without agency, calculation, or judgment. Finally, Hénaff offers something of a counterposition, in tune with Ricoeur's hermeneutics of oneself-as-another, where giver and receiver are legitimately acknowledged as mutual beneficiaries of the gifting process—a position where reciprocity is key again.

Contesting the deconstructive claim that for a gift to be a gift, the giver must be unaware of giving and the receiver unaware of the giver's identity, Hénaff responds that we must learn from the original meanings of the gift in concrete social anthropologies—namely, the power to bring selves and strangers together and overcome enmity in the name of peace.[8] That is what the so-called potlatch was all about. The conversion of hostility into hospitality. Drawing on Ricoeur's hermeneutics of dialogue, Hénaff concludes that possible reciprocity, rather than impossible disinterestedness, is at the root of genuine gift rituals and institutions, forming social and political bonds between otherwise competing actors. As such, the gift is the precondition of all functioning societies. And this recognition of the fundamental function of the gift calls in turn for a proper philosophy of hospitality, where host and guest are afforded equal dignity and agency. The present volume is a modest attempt to apply these continental conversations about possible/impossible gifts to relevant questions of hospitality for our time.

Toward a Gift Economy

In a piece entitled "Humanity and Hospitality: An Approach to Theology in Times of Migration" (2018), René Dausner relates the continental debates on hospitality to concerns about immigration, power, and fear.[9] His aim is to explore moral and religious contributions to the topic in light of Europe's migration crisis. He rightly states: "Migration, that is to say the movement of people who have lost nearly everything except their bare life and who come to Europe in the hope of improvement, is one of the biggest ethical, political, and theological challenges of today."[10] Dausner frames his argument through the lens of recent protectionist practices in the upsurge of neonationalist movements in Europe, which, he argues, find their roots in the fear and scapegoating of the other. And this also applies to the United States, as evidenced by the populist influence of alt-right attitudes toward refugees and international trade, as well as an alarming disregard (under Trump) about climate change, among other global humanitarian crises.

Dausner rehearses the standard debate between "conditional" and "unconditional" hospitality, observing how for the former the host remains host and the guest remains guest. "The host remains the master of the house, the country, the nation, he controls the threshold, he controls the borders, and when he welcomes the guest he wants to keep the mastery."[11] In other words, many hosts never fully relinquish "control" or "power" over the situation—cautiously keeping guests at a distance, despite letting them into their house. Kant's observation about hospitality in his classic "Perpetual Peace" essay—canonical for all modern discussions of the topic—conforms to this cautious model (at least by Derrida's account). Insofar as the guest behaves peaceably, the guest is granted the right to appear—that is, to *visit*; however, the guest is by no means granted the right to *stay*. This is to say that the rights of the guest end with the capacity to appear, but again, *only if* they behave peaceably. Thus, hospitality is conditioned by the disposition of the guest in the home of the host, contingent upon established house rules—a situation that obtains in the German state's hosting of foreign workers (*Gastarbeiter*).

A crucial point here is that Kant's rationale is by no means grounded in xenophobia, but guided by a quite practical sense of prudence: without a mutual recognition of the dignity of each other (the host included), the risk of pure hospitality is total impracticality, and therefore, by default, war. Kant's account will be more thoroughly addressed in Part II, since there is perhaps more "unconditionality" in Kant's position than meets the eye—especially when analyzed through the lens of moral psychology, and what type of disposition is involved in exercising the *universal* principle of right. To be "universal" is, generally speaking, to lack particular or partisan conditions.

Unconditional hospitality involves opening the door to the guest without question—even at the risk of the stranger "coming and destroying the place, initiating a revolution, stealing everything, or killing everyone" (Derrida).[12] This means that one's door is actually open to whoever happens to enter, and with whatever motives they might have. It is marked by pure, radical openness. By Derrida's account, unconditional hospitality is vital, because it serves as the condition for hospitality itself, for in order that hospitality exist, there has to be an absolute opening. It has to be unconditional and therefore *impossible*, that is, openly oriented toward the new, the unknown, the yet-to-come—what Derrida calls the "messianic."[13] We find here again the reasoning of the gift: hospitality of course being nothing other than the gift of one's house, one's bread, and perhaps above all, one's self. But what, specifically, makes the messianic welcome impossible?

For Derrida, unconditional hospitality is marked by the transgression of all laws, rules, and grammars. It is—echoing Johannes de Silencio in *Fear and Trembling*—a teleological suspension of the "ethical," that is, a relinquishing of the universal moral law—grounded in pure reason (Kant and Hegel)—for the sake of a higher end that somehow preserves the moral law in its execution. This paradox is not a cognizable contract or conversation, but rather a radical exposure. That is, an unconditional surrendering of oneself. Pure rupture. A blind leap. A form of faith. What Derrida and Caputo call "madness."

Dausner ultimately follows Ricoeur in taking issue with the deconstructive model of *pure* hospitality, calling for another, more practicable understanding that does not forsake the law of hospitality itself: namely, "hermeneutical" or "linguistic" hospitality, that is, a type of hospitality rooted in conversation, exchange, negotiation—finding a common ground. This type of hospitality is not only possible but ethical. While conceding that hospitality always entails a risk, it seeks to protect certain occasions in which the host truly ought to say "no," since this is both reasonable and responsible; and it requires the courage to discern (e.g., between violent invaders and needy refugees). These points will be fleshed out in both parts of this volume.

Dausner concludes by invoking Levinas's account of ethics and the religious experience of the alterity of the other—understood by Levinas as the *irruption* of the impossible in the possible. And here he also cites the Greek counterpart to hospitality, *philoxenia*, which entails not only hospitality to strangers, but *love of the strange*: a love that is "understood as an imitation of God." This in keeping with Matthew 25: "For I was hungry and you gave me food; I was thirsty and you gave me drink; I was a stranger and you took me in. . . . Assuredly, I say to you, inasmuch as you did it to one of the least of these my brethren, you did it to me." In hospitality, by this reading, we approach God (in the image of God, given by God)—paradoxically bridging the gap between the possible and the impossible.

In a series of analyses in his *Action and Contemplation* series (2019), Richard Rohr further explores the theological aspects of hospitality in relation to what he calls a "gift economy." Paralleling the debates on gift, giving, and givenness in continental phenomenology, Rohr and fellow theologians apply the question of the gift to a discussion of a sacred economy of sufficiency and hospitality versus a capitalist economy of scarcity and competition. One of the virtues of such analyses is to provide a material contextuality regarding particular empirical goods that sometimes remain abstract, if not actually "bracketed," in phenomenological studies.

A gift economy is one that challenges the dominant ideology of consumer capitalism. It promises a departure from free enterprise market systems based on competition, scarcity, and greed in favor of a countercultural economy based on social interaction. Such a postconsumer economy of the gift promotes a covenant that serves the common good. While a purely mercantile system violates neighborly relations by stratifying power relations according to money, self-interest, investment, entitlement, and surplus, the gift economy advocates a relationship to goods as gifts that circulate between interchangeable hosts and guests. This creates a social space where monetary exchange—where everything and everyone is treated as a "commodity"—becomes a process of reciprocal hospitality between citizens enjoying rights of equal opportunity and distribution. It opens a space where strangers become neighbors.

In such an alternative "sacred" economy, hospitality becomes a practical moral value operating with a chorus of collaborating agents—from food hubs and cooperatives to communal social enterprises, climate change movements, and health and education activism. Within the framework of such an ethic of hospitality, neighborliness ceases to be some nostalgic remnant of bygone days and becomes an indispensable value for human flourishing in the present and the future. It recognizes that the free market consumer ideology has produced a deep social disorder—dating back to the economic policies of "enclosure" (the privatizing of common land) and "capital" (the centralizing of wealth into the hands of the few while monetizing every human person as a "wage earner" with "use," "exchange," and "surplus" value). So where the market ideology commercializes everything at an impersonal national or global level, the gift economy proposes a countermove toward the restoration of "the commons"—a shared culture of reciprocity serving the common good, understood as common health, wealth, nourishment, education, and justice.[14]

While the hospitality ethic argues there is always enough for everyone—if properly distributed and circulated—the scarcity model claims there is never enough. The former sponsors an ethics of shared collaboration and contribution over an analytics of competition and calculation. The mindset of scarcity sees things as objects to be coveted and acquired rather than as gifts to be received and passed on in a circle of sufficiency. And sufficiency here does not mean a quantity or amount of anything but rather a sense that there is *more* than enough to go around, if justice be done. It is all a matter of existential set and setting: "When we live in the context of sufficiency, we find a natural freedom and integrity. We engage in life from a sense of our own wholeness rather than a desperate longing to be complete. We feel naturally called to share the resources that flow through our lives—our time, our money, our wisdom, our energy, at whatever level those resources flow—to serve our highest commitment." From this comes the conviction that "sufficiency as a way of being offers us enormous personal freedom and possibility."[15]

An economy of hospitality, in sum, is one that values abundance over affluence, gratuity over greed, compassion over unfettered consumption, goods over commodities. Rohr cites the following critique of free enterprise capitalism: "While it is good at generating wealth is it is not so good at spreading it around . . . the profit motif appeals to our acquisitive nature. It nourishes greed and can make us callous to the suffering of others. . . . Left to its own devices, free enterprise capitalism would ruin the environment and let people starve . . . (so) while it may be a remarkable engine for driving economic growth, an engine is not the same as a steering wheel."[16] The steering wheel, Richard Rohr and Arthur Simon agree, should be a gift economy based on public justice and affording priority to the principle of sufficiency over scarcity.

Ironically, one of the theological virtues of gift economies is not only to restore a positive incarnate "materiality" of giving and receiving, hosting and guesting, but also to confirm some of the most radical material findings of modern science. For contrary to a conventional scientific understanding of nature as competitive, more recent discoveries of astrophysics and microphysics reveal a powerful role for mutuality, synergy, coexistence, and cooperation. Survival of the fittest is being replaced with survival of the most hospitable![17] So what might first appear as a mere utopian ideal or messianic promise is in fact a view of things that consorts with the deepest workings of our physical universe. A gift economy may not be so "impossible" after all.

A Postapocalyptic Culture of Welcome

In her book *Hospitality in a Time of Terror: Strangers at the Gate* (2018), Lindsay Balfour approaches the subject of immigrants from a cultural, rather than theological or economic perspective. She probes hospitality in a post-9/11 world, underlining the dialectic of hosts and guests in a variety of cultural productions, including film, literature, art, and public memorials—a point that will be explored in some detail in Part I of this volume. She asks: "What does the post-9/11 cultural archive suggest about ways we engage or disengage with in the lives of others, and how might these texts and artifacts bring us closer to an understanding of both the possibilities and the dangers of hospitality now?"[18]

In conversation with Edward Casey, Balfour opens with a moving description of "Strangers Gate" in Central Park, which is an entrance to the park commemorating and paying homage to the history of immigration in New York City.[19] Unique to the United States—especially in cosmopolitan spaces like New York City or Los Angeles—is the fact that the "nonnative" status of its "citizens" is almost ubiquitous. What does it really mean to be a "native" in the United States? The United States is among the most heterogeneous countries in the world, comprising immigrants from every corner of the globe, a country founded by those fleeing various forms of persecution, ultimately in search of a better life, opportunity, and above all, freedom. It seems reasonable to suggest, along with Balfour, that in a strong sense almost all North Americans are "nonnatives"—a point one ought to remind oneself of in the wake of gated communities, advanced security systems, and conservative discourses demanding a *bigger and better* wall at the southern border. We currently live in an age marked by acts of violence and hate that are fueled by xenophobia—a phobia that frequently finds its roots in radical misunderstandings. These misunderstandings are often grounded in a lack of "conversation"—a point we hope to address in the present volume, suggesting conversation is the moment when hospitality in theory turns to hospitality in practice.

Balfour rightly claims that hospitality is anything but a uniform phenomenon: "hospitality has never been a stable, uncontested, or purely altruistic figure. What hospitality *is* is an intricate structure of ethics, violence, promise, threat, and impossibility that has been worked through, tested, and struggled over for millennia."[20] Much like a "Platonic form," hospitality is something that we all *know*, at least to some extent; but the moment we try to capture it, to delimit it, to define it, it falls through our finger tips—and we are left wrestling with the interplay between its unconditional and conditional manifestations. What we know perhaps even better than what hospitality *is* is what hospitality is *not*: closing borders, refusing to grant asylum to those fleeing genocide, and asking the vital questions: Am I really my brother's keeper? Why is a stranger my problem? What do I owe strangers who finds their roots beyond my nation's borders? The crucial point here, we argue in this volume, is that each and every one of us, at some time or another, has been *both* guest and host. Hospitality is built into the very fabric of who we are. Beginning with birth, we are hosted, nurtured, cared for, guested.

In the same vein, Krista Tippett conducted a revealing dialogue with Cuban American engineer and poet Richard Blanco, who, as an immigrant himself (coming to America from Cuba by way of Spain), has spent much time meditating on the meaning of place, home, exile, refuge, and belonging. When asked where he finds hope and joy in what many describe as an era of despair, closed doors, and hostility toward the stranger, he responds:

> One of the most beautiful things that I see, and it happened first with the ban on Muslims and whatnot, that people, at least in my lifetime, for the first time, were standing up for something that didn't affect them directly. That is a democracy. . . . We are stepping up and realizing that the quality of life, the virtue of this country, depends on every human being's story, to a certain degree; that our happiness depends on other people's happiness, and we're moving from a space of dependence to realizing our interdependence.[21]

Existentially speaking, hospitality, grounded in this sense of interdependence—echoing recent discoveries in physics pointing toward collaboration rather than competition—is simply part of our constitution. And it often reveals itself in the face of radical injustice, such as in the Trump administration's immigration ban in 2017. It is in such moments of despair that we cannot help but find ourselves drawn toward the other-as-oneself, pulled by a "fraternity" that is always and already the case. That is, drawn toward others who are in fact strangers, but are nonetheless worth speaking and fighting for. Daily images of such fraternity from around the world are a testimony to the intrinsic desire we have to host, protect, include, and be with others.

The dialogue ends with a reading from Blanco's "Declaration of Interdependence," which opens his book *How to Love a Country*. The end of the piece is worth quoting in full:

> We hold these truths to be self-evident . . . We're the cure for hatred caused by despair. We're the good morning of a bus driver who remembers our name, the tattooed man who gives up his seat on the subway. We're every door held open with a smile when we look into each other's eyes the way we behold the moon. We're the moon. We're the promise of one people, one breath declaring to one another: I see you. I need you. I am you.[22]

Although it might be true, as Blanco points out, that we are the cure for hatred caused by despair, we cannot deny that we are also the cause. And here again we return to the core debate between conditional and unconditional hospitality—and hospitality's ostensible impossibility. The challenge is to find a middle way between a model of calculated exchange and a hyperbolic model of incalculable rupture. For hospitality to be hospitality, we need a special kind of "symmetrical asymmetry" where each person gives more than she receives and receives more than she gives—without why. A reciprocity of nonreciprocity between host and guest. Where host and guest become interchangeable without ever losing their inimitable, unique singularity. Hospitality does not occur in a market place where things are bought and sold in contractual negotiations of supply and demand, credit and debit, scarcity and surplus. Real hospitality occurs beyond the walls of economic calculation; it is not about who owes each other what but about what is beyond investment and debt.

This renders hospitality a rather frightening experience, at times, because one cannot always anticipate what is to come—among the most terrifying of possibilities being the emptying of the self before the solicitation of the other. But, as we hope to show below, with death often comes birth—to borrow Hannah Arendt's term, *natality*—meaning that hospitality's *deconstruction* of the self frequently entails a *reconstruction* of both the self and the other. Part II will probe why this process—the disruption of oneself by the other—is, psychologically speaking, so terrifying, and will attempt to unravel what precisely makes it appear so impossible, and in what sense that impossibility is nonetheless possible.

In kilter with Balfour's timely study, this volume seeks to work through and beyond theoretical quandaries of deconstruction and rethink questions of the "stranger" *in practice*. This means engaging with hospitality through the arts and media more than ever in a "culture of fear" framed by the threat of anthropogenic climate change.[23] The question of ecological change is also one of hospitality. How do we host nonhuman others? How do we honor our role as guests on this earth, as shepherds and stewards of its endangered species—animal, mineral, and vegetal? This discussion is central to an environmental ethics of hospitality toward trees, rivers, ecosystems, and all sentient beings that now find themselves in increasing danger. As sea levels inevitably rise, those displaced from homes that have been swallowed by the oceans will simply have no place to go. This is to say that they will have no choice but to "knock on their neighbor's door," asking for food, water, and refuge. But what will it take to open the door?

Our ultimate aim in this volume is to apply text to action, that is, to translate philosophies of hospitality into some concrete examples drawn from our contemporary world, especially relative to issues of conflict resolution, cathartic commemoration, interconfessional dialogue, and, finally, classroom pedagogy regarding immigration, diversity, tolerance, and peace.

Presentation of Parts and Chapters

A word about the composition of this volume: Part I, "Four Faces of Hospitality: Linguistic, Narrative, Confessional, Carnal," written by Richard Kearney, discusses recent research on the philosophy of hospitality, which informs the international Guestbook Project he directs (www.guestbook project.org). This first part articulates an ethics of hosting the stranger in four short chapters. Opening with an account of linguistic hospitality, advanced by Paul Ricoeur and Jacques Derrida, it goes on to illustrate how this model of hospitality as translation and narrative exchange applies to three recent pedagogical experiments: the Guestbook Project of exchanging stories, the Twinsome Minds project of "Double Remembrance," and the "Exchanging Memories" project of the Irish Famine Memorial in New York. The discussion then reviews debates on religious hospitality as translation in contemporary political philosophy—notably in critical theory and Jürgen Habermas—before concluding with a plea for a "double hospitality" involving both word and touch. The ultimate aim here is to explore bridges between "linguistic" and "carnal" ways of hosting the stranger, an exploration that culminates with a promissory note on political hospitality, serving as prelude to Part II.

Part II, "Hospitality and Moral Psychology: Exploring the Border between Theory and Practice," written by Melissa Fitzpatrick, builds on the insights gleaned in Part I. It analyzes the relationship between hospitality and moral psychology (namely, how we understand ourselves and our moral motivations) in four further chapters. This second part begins with a careful hermeneutic of Kant's classic notion of international hospitality in relation to the experience of respect/obeying the moral law (Chapter 5). From there, it provides discussion of the post-Kantian shift to philosophies of hospitality—in particular that of Emmanuel Levinas—elucidating the Derrida/Ricoeur/Kearney debate on impossible and possible hospitality discussed in Part I. It concludes with a consideration of Arendt's more political/practical position, offering a middle way between Kant and Levinas (Chapter 6).

Chapter 7 offers an analysis of the practical reclamation of Aristotelian virtue ethics in contemporary Anglo-American debates, arguing for a reading of *phronesis* that involves hospitality to the unknown and to others, engaging Talbot Brewer's recent reimagining of virtue ethics. In light of the account in Part I of narrative hospitality's experiments in contemporary culture, Chapter 8 explores some pedagogical applications that follow from the preceding chapters, briefly abstracting what a pedagogy of hospitality might entail, drawing on the author's own work in precollege philosophy in the Mississippi Delta and on the border of the United States and Mexico.

This volume ultimately suggests that an ethics of radical hospitality—which takes the route of embracing complexity, diversity, and ambiguity—happens, first and foremost, by opening oneself in narrative exchange to someone or something other than oneself. That is, something new that we have not seen, encountered, or experienced before. This invariably involves crossing borders, both literally and figuratively. That is, national and domestic borders, as well as the borders of what we know and hold with certainty. We understand this to be what sits at the heart of a narrative peace pedagogy without borders, which informs all of Guestbook Project's endeavors.

What we hope to suggest is that despite our propensity to cling in fear to certain and familiar dogmas there is another way: namely, to follow the intrinsic human desire to wager with the unknown, leap into the unanticipated and venture the strange. In so doing, we not only learn to understand ourselves as hosts—exposed, vulnerable, daring to share a world with others—but also that fostering a disposition of hospitality toward what is other than ourselves is part of a full and flourishing life.

Beyond this, we contend that an essential condition for the possibility of overcoming war and the xenophobia that often fuels it, is to engage in the often uncomfortable activity of narrative exchange that embraces difference and distinction, takes the risk of not knowing what is true with a capital T, and has the courage to trade one's cherished gods with the gods of others. It signals an audacity to embrace the new by "chancing one's arm," opening a vital space for unheard voices and welcoming strangers to our home.

We would like to think of this book not only as a philosophical companion piece to our practical work in Guestbook and the classroom, but also as a companion volume to two previous publications on the topic: *Hosting the Stranger: Between Religions* (2011), edited by Richard Kearney and James Taylor, which explores the cardinal role of hospitality in five major wisdom traditions (Judaism, Christianity, Islam, Buddhism and Hinduism); and *Phenomenology of the Stranger: Between Hostility and Hospitality* (2011), edited by Richard Kearney and Kascha Semonovitch, which investigates the relationship between hostility and hospitality from a variety of hermeneutic perspectives. While these two books laid the platforms of interreligious and phenomenological dialogue for a new understanding of hospitality, the present volume attempts to *apply* this understanding to concrete living examples of pedagogy, art, and commemoration in the contemporary moral world. It aims to show that the ultimate end of hospitality is the practice of peace.

PART | I |

Four Faces of Hospitality
Linguistic, Narrative, Confessional, Carnal

RICHARD KEARNEY

1

Linguistic Hospitality
The Risk of Translation

Linguistic hospitality promotes translation as a mediation between host and guest languages. There is a double duty here: to remain faithful to one's own language and to welcome the foreigner's language at the same time.

This double duty entails important ethical responsibilities. It is a challenge we can fail by succumbing to one of two temptations. First, there is the danger of absorbing the Other into the Same, assimilating the singular differences of the guest tongue to the totalizing norms of the host tongue. This makes for a bad translation, and at a moral and political level can lead to extremes of linguistic chauvinism, xenophobia, or imperialism. Second, there exists the contrary temptation to surrender one's own linguistic dwelling completely to the incoming Other, to the point where there is no host at home at all to receive a guest in the first place. This capitulation can lead to supine servility to an overwhelming or oppressive Other. To avoid the two dialectical extremes—of either linguistic hegemony or humiliation—one may take a middle road of linguistic hospitality where one honors the host and guest languages equitably. Paul Ricoeur spells out the far-reaching implications of such linguistic hospitality in *On Translation*—implications that range from the literary and ontological to the ethical and religious:

> Translation sets us not only intellectual work . . . but also an ethical problem. Bringing the reader to the author, bringing the author to the reader, at the risk of serving and of betraying two masters: this is

to practice what I like to call linguistic hospitality. It is this which serves as a model for other forms of hospitality that I think resemble it: confessions, religions, are they not like languages that are foreign to one another, with their lexicon, their grammar, their rhetoric, their style which we must learn in order to make our way into them? And is Eucharistic hospitality not to be taken up with the same risks of translation-betrayal, but also with the same renunciation of the perfect translation.[1]

A crucial step in resisting the lure of the Perfect Translation is to observe a delicate balance between proximity (welcoming the stranger into our midst) and distance (accepting that something is always lost in translation: the other's meanings and allusions are never completely ours). We can aim for the most approximate equivalences and correspondences, but we can never assume these to be adequate. Translation is always an endless task. It is a "working through"—analogous to a psychoanalytic *Durcharbeitung*—where the labor of translation between one linguistic world and another involves some element of mourning: a letting go of the egocentric drive to reduce the alterity of the guest to our own fantasies. Such fantasies are based on the falsehood that, in translation, there exists only one true language: one's own.

But as Ricoeur repeatedly insists, there is no such thing as language, only languages. Linguistic hospitality is always in the plural. Or as the old adage goes, *Traditore, tradutore*: to translate is always in some sense to betray—meaning we all live "after Babel." And this is no bad thing. Our linguistic fallenness marks a basic finitude that saves us from the illusion of returning to some prelapsarian *logos* (where we play God speaking a language with a perfect word for a perfect thing). And it also deflates the lure of a perfect *logos* of the future—such as the enlightenment dream of a *caracteristica universalis* or a pan-European Esperanto. The translation paradigm of hospitality resists such delusions and resists historical projects to impose a single language of Empire—Greek, Latin, French, Spanish, English—on a multiplicity of diverse vernaculars. It is the right of every living language to be translated into another language while also retaining certain untranslatable intimacies and opacities. Every tongue has its secrets. All speech casts a shadow. Whence the legitimate double injunction of every guest language when faced with a host: "Translate me! Don't translate me!" Render me, but not completely. Good translation is transfusion, not fusion. It signals a transition between two, never a reduction to one. It is a dialogical welcoming of difference (*dia-legein*), offering a passageway between the Scylla of abstract universalism and the Charybdis of narrow parochialism.

Good translation renounces the claim to self-sufficiency, acknowledging that we share words as we share clothes. To paraphrase Ricoeur, we are called to make our language don the garments of strangers while simultaneously inviting strangers to step into the fabric of our speech. Translation is transvestitude from the word go, from Babel on. In the beginning was hermeneutics—namely, the interpretation of diverse meanings, tongues, intentions, and lexicons. *In principio fuit interpres*. There is no pure pristine *logos*, unless it is God's, and we are not gods. To be human is to interpret and to interpret is to translate. There never was a human being without an Other, a host without a guest. Adam had Eve and Eve had Adam. In the beginning was hospitality—and, as we shall see, hostility.

Thus understood, translation involves a recognition of our human fallibility, keeping us open to the never-ending task of *more* translation, again and again. The only criterion of a good translation is another translation. Which is why the great classics are both untranslatable and infinitely translatable. (There are never enough renditions of Homer or Shakespeare.) We are dealing with a drama of fragile hospitality. Ricoeur puts it well: "Despite the conflictual character which renders the task of the translator dramatic, he or she will find satisfaction in what I would like to call linguistic hospitality. Its predicament is that of a correspondence without complete adhesion. This is a fragile condition, which admits of no verification other than a new translation . . . to translate afresh after the translation."[2] And, Ricoeur adds, extending the paradigm of translatability to narrativity in general: "Just as in a narration it is always possible to tell the story in a different way, likewise in translation it is always possible to translate otherwise, without ever hoping to bridge the gap between equivalence and perfect adhesion. Linguistic hospitality is the act of inhabiting the word of the Other paralleled by the act of receiving the word of the Other into one's own home, one's own dwelling."[3] But the host can never capture the guest in its house. The guest must sometimes take leave in order to remain a guest. And the host must sometimes release the guest in order to remain a host. There is an "untranslatable kernel" in every translation that reminds us that host and guest languages are never the same— and never should be.

While this acknowledgment of irreducible linguistic difference entails a therapeutic dissolving of the fallacy of fusion, it opens up the challenge of plurality and natality. (For natality read: wonder, surprise, the shock of the new—a point that will be further elaborated in Part II.) It is precisely when two distinct tongues cross that a third may be born. And this birthing can be multiple, we noted, in the countless translations of the great classics—Greek, Sanskrit, Latin, Hebrew—into numerous languages and then further versions of each vernacular language. We do not lament the serial renditions of Virgil or Proust, for example; we celebrate them. And the same goes for a text like the Bible, running from the Septuagint translation from Hebrew into Greek to Jerome's translation into Latin, and the great vernacular of King James into English, of Luther and Buber into German, of Chouraqui into French, and so on. With each translation, a "semantic surplus" is created by the fertile collision of separate language. Something new is born that is mutually enhancing for both cultures. Think of how, for instance, in the Septuagint translation of Exodus 3:15—"I am who may be"—the Greek ontological notion of being (*ontos on*) as formal and material substance is radically transformed by the Hebrew notion of God as a promise of historical and eschatological becoming. And vice versa. So by the time Maimonides is writing his Hebraic-Hellenic metaphysics in *Guide for the Perplexed*, both Greeks and Jews are reinterpreting their respective notions of what it means to *be* in the world—a bicultural crossing that opens radically novel ways of rethinking personhood, time, eternity, relation, finitude. After the babel of multiple translations, we may say with James Joyce that "Greekjew is Jewgreek." Athens and Jerusalem are never the same again. And a similar point could be made about Paul's translations from Hebrew and Aramaic into Greek in his Epistles or the early Church Fathers in their mystical theologies of "being beyond being." Christian Neoplatonism and Patristic mysticism offer new hermeneutic wagers regarding the meaning of existence. (This argument extends, of course, beyond the Abrahamic-Hellenic traditions to the great translations of the Upanishads or the Buddhist Heart Sutra or other wisdom literatures.)

But let's be careful: translation is not always on the side of the angels. Each transition between self and stranger involves the possibility of mistranslation. All understanding contains misunderstanding, as the hermeneutic adage goes. Hostility to the Other is as real an option as hospitality. Not to mention ordinary mortal mistakenness. Emile Benveniste observes in *Language and Indo-European Society* that hospitality and hostility share the same root, *hostis*, which can mean both host and guest, both friend and enemy.[4] Hence, the notion of translation as a dramatic event—a task, a risk, a wager between hostility (reducing the guest to the same) and hospitality (acknowledging the irreducible gap between oneself and another). This is why Antoine Berman speaks of translation as "*l'épreuve de l'étranger*"—an existential testing or trial of the stranger.[5] This notion of *épreuve* calls in turn for a special kind of practical wisdom or judgment (*phronesis*): namely, the ability to discern between varying calls and demands of the stranger—as foreigner or immigrant, as alien or refugee, as adversary or invader. Hence the constant wagering between hostility and hospitality, between vigilance and welcome: an oscillation that Derrida names with the neologism "hostipitality." Moreover, the capacity to navigate between distinct persons and perspectives is something that operates not just *interlinguistically* (between a native and foreign tongue) but also *intralinguistically* (between speaking beings within the same tongue). The mother tongue has many infants. Indeed, as psychoanalysis shows, translation is often at work between our conscious and unconscious selves. We frequently find ourselves foreigners within our own *langue maternelle*—and within the depths of our own psyches. We are, deep down, as Kristeva reminds us, strangers to ourselves.[6]

Jacques Derrida makes a radical point here about the "impossibility" of pure hospitality. Every translation, he argues, risks some degree of hostility toward the other in so far as it asks the Other to render itself in terms of one's own projects, prejudices, and perspectives. We naturally read every stranger with respect to our lifeworld of cultural horizons. As soon as I, *qua* host, ask, "Who are you?" my guest is obliged to respond in my terms. All hermeneutics in practice is a mixed act of "hostipitality"—welcoming the other at the same time as one translates its alterity into someone "like me": a self I can recognize and identify. Though Ricoeur interprets this "like" in term of someone similar (*semblable*) rather than someone the same (*même*) as myself, Derrida holds the deconstructive line that any need for similarity is already a compromising of the strangeness of the Stranger. (This, by Derrida's own admission, is a radicalization of Husserl's phenomenological analysis of knowing others in his Fifth Cartesian Meditation.)

So we might sum up the difference between Ricoeur and Derrida thus: where the hermeneutics of translation practices conditional hospitality (which involves some interpretive judgment regarding mixed bags of "hostipitality"), deconstruction calls for unconditional hospitality where I accept the Other regardless of its origin or identity—human, animal, or divine. Pure hospitality, Derrida insists, does not ask for IDs or passports; it is not concerned with border controls or contracts but invites pure exposure to alterity, welcoming the stranger "without why." If there is a knock at the door, you open it without asking if it is a messiah or a monster. Once you put hospitality into laws, rules, and norms, you take the risk out of it, you compromise the radical daring of undecidability, the yes to all that comes. Derrida is undaunted. "Let us say yes to who or what turns up," he writes in *Of Hospitality*, "before any determination, or anticipation, whether or not it is to do with a foreigner, an immigrant, an uninvited guest, or an unexpected visitor, whether or not the new arrival is the citizen of another country, a human, animal or divine creature, a living or dead thing, male or female."[7] In short, absolute hospitality welcomes the stranger independently of all legal, political, or epistemological conventions, calling for a pure leap of faith toward the "absolutely other." Or, as Derrida puts it in his inimitably hyperbolic way, "every other is absolutely other" (*tout autre est tout autre*). The stranger is always, at bottom, absolutely strange. And no stranger is excluded.

Now, most would agree that such "pure" hospitality is not possible in terms of everyday practice—where the only feasible form of welcome is always contingent upon this or that set of conditions. Absolute unconditional hospitality is "impossible," but it is, Derrida insists, no less "desirable" for all that; although to most people it may seem "blind," "mad," or "mystical"—a mere "dream."[8] Any attempt to make the impossible possible is already a matter of betrayal, compromise, and contagion. Where hermeneutic hospitality speaks of *conversion* between host and guest, deconstructive hospitality speaks of *contamination*. This explains Ricoeur's confession that the difference between the two approaches is that between the words "difficult" and "impossible."[9]

There is, I think, a fundamental tension at work here between a phenomenology of alterity (Levinas and Derrida) and a hermeneutics of empathy (Ricoeur). The first insists on the absolute, irreducible difference of the Other—and implies that any reduction to "sameness" or even a positing of "similarity" is by definition unjust. The second proposes the development of sympathy and imagination through listening to the other's story and identifying with it. This is exacerbated by a further tension between the call for justice (here I stand) on the one hand, and the call for openness and endless translatability (there is always something more) on the other. To some extent, this has been a crucial tension at the heart of continental philosophy for much of the twentieth century, one that I have endeavored to address in previous works like *Strangers, Gods, and Monsters* and that is evidenced in the two parts of this volume: Part I on the side of a hermeneutics of narrative empathy, Part II on the side of an alterity of rupture.

This tension raises the following complex question: Is *any* version of similarity between self and other always a mode of hostility? And is it really credible to claim that the stranger is always absolutely and unknowably strange? Are there not *many* kinds and degrees of strangeness, which we need to tactfully and carefully acknowledge? Indeed, might not the claim that the other is truly absolutely other—sharing nothing in common with me at all—even function as a form of *hostility*, if taken too far? I think it unwise to assume that any form of similarity is *necessarily* more hostile than any form of difference, as Levinas and Derrida seem to insist. Xenophobia, for example, often arises out of an obssession with the stranger's otherness, giving rise to hostility and violence. A fear that may be sometimes overcome by realizing that the other actually shares many similar hopes, dreams, fears as myself—which becomes evident, for example, through reading narratives from other cultures. This recognition of the other as someone *like* myself, who shares important things in common with me, does not necessarily result in appropriating or colonializing moves—but often the contrary. Much of colonialism has been undergirded precisely by the presupposition that the colonized were thoroughly *other* than their conquerors. This is the infamous lure of "Orientalism."

I would argue that empathy always requires some sense of "likeness," some feeling "with" (*sym-pathein*) that assumes at least a basic minimum of similarity between me and the other. A sense that—as I hear the story of the other—some part of me can say, "That is my story too." (I return to this in the next chapter, and it will be further addressed in Part II through the lens of Arendt.) In such instances of linguistic sharing, my translation of the other's words is not seen as a form of hostility, but the opposite. Translation—as mutual transfer between different minds—involves some element of appropriation: namely, receiving the other as a self *like me* in some respects, while remaining *other than me* in other respects. Empathy is vital to community, even if one must be wary of empathizing too much—to the point of believing one *is* the other and can see things precisely as they do, denying the unique singularity of their experience. Language hinges on some assumed common ground—and without it, there is no communion. If you cannot empathize with the suffering of the dispossessed, what hope is there for any ethics worthy of the name?

Last, a scruple about the claim for infinite translatability. One has to admit that there is no guarantee that having as many interpretations as possible will, of itself, *necessarily* result in a more ethical attitude (though it is a possibility). And, more troubling still, if there are endless more or less equal ways of retelling the stories and if this diversity were to be applauded for its own sake, it would be hard to claim any better or worse translation at all. Some critical nuance is called for here—a middle way between translatability and untranslatability, that is, between hospitality understood as empathic conversation on the one hand and as endless dissemination of readings, on the other. In what follows we will be seeking to turn ostensible contradictions into fertile tensions, applying the middle way of hospitality to a series of examples drawn from contemporary culture and politics.

2

Narrative Hospitality
Three Pedagogical Experiments

In this second chapter, I explore the possibility of an ethics of hospitality in relation to three practical examples: the Guestbook Project of exchanging stories, the Twinsome Minds project of double remembrance, and the Irish Famine Memorial project of crossed commemoration. All three draw from my own "hermeneutic belonging" to Irish cultural history.

But first a word on the hermeneutics of narrative hospitality. In his topical text, "Reflections on a new Ethos for Europe" (1996/2004), Paul Ricoeur extends the model of linguistic hospitality more concretely to what he calls "narrative hospitality." He describes this as "taking responsibility in imagination and in sympathy for the story of the other, through the life narratives which concern the other."[1] In the case of memorials this assumes the form of exchanges between different national or collective histories as we practice an art of transference allowing us to welcome the story of our neighbor or adversary. For one nation's narrative of glory is often another's narrative of suffering. Victors and victims need to exchange places by exchanging stories. And exchanging stories is already an invitation to change history: to reanimate forgotten stories out of our "debt to the dead."

We will return to the ethics of narrative hospitality in our discussions of memory in the third section of this chapter, but let us summarize here three key characteristics:

Narrative Plurality: Every story can be told from a variety of perspectives. Multiple readings of historic events—e.g., the French Revolution, the Irish Famine, the discovery of America—do not spell a lack of respect for the singularity of these events. On the contrary, it may well be that it is the very diversity of narrative accounts which honors the inexhaustibly rich character of the very pastness and foreignness of each historical moment. Recounting differently may, paradoxically, serve as guarantor for a deeper appreciation of the unique specificity and strangeness of such moments. "The ability to recount the founding events of a national history in different ways is reinforced by the exchange of cultural memories. This capacity to exchange has as a touchstone the will to share symbolically and respectfully in the commemoration of the founding events of other national cultures, as well as those of their ethnic minorities and their minority religious denominations."[2] And, one might add, such commemorations apply as much to moments of trauma as to moments of glory. There is a hermeneutic risk involved in every interpretation of history—and an ethical awareness of the justice and injustice at issue. History is never innocent. There are almost always victors and victims and the power and permission to narrate is not given to everyone equally. Hence the need for many stories and the obligation to keep on telling them.

Narrative Transformation: The historical past can be revisited in terms of unexperienced or unexplored "possibilities," thereby giving a future to the past. As Ricoeur puts it, "the past is a cemetery of promises which have not been kept." Narrative hospitality is a way of retelling untold stories so as to realize such promissory notes, "bringing them back to life, like the dry bones in the valley described in the prophecy of Ezekiel."[3] Here the hermeneutic model of memory meets the cathartic model of healing. We shall explore specific instances of narrative remembrance below.

Narrative Pardon: By empathizing with others though narrative exchange, we can work through the wounds of the past so as to open up moments of charity and gift.[4] This involves moving beyond a contractual reciprocity of exchange to an incalculable order of charity—a leap that transcends the rules of justice in the name of "something more": namely, forgiving the enemy and "shattering the debt." Here law is supplemented by love. And in this bold step toward a poetics of pardon there comes a point where a narrative exchange—of histories, memories, testimonies—often needs to be supplemented by action. Narrative hospitality calls for performative hospitality. Text turns to act. Word becomes gesture.[5]

We will return to these points in more detail below. Now to our three examples.

Guestbook: Exchanging Stories, Changing Histories

The Guestbook Project was founded in 2009 as a scholarly experiment in narrative hospitality. It began as an interdisciplinary seminar focusing on the theme of "Hosting the Stranger: Between Hostility and Hospitality." The project was intellectually inspired by the fact that, in most Indo-European languages, the word for "guest" and "enemy" is the same—for example, *hostis* in Latin is the common root of both "hostility" and "hospitality." So too for *xenos* in Greek (xenophobia and xenophilia), *Gast* in Old German (friendly guest or ghastly enemy), and so on. The aim of Guestbook was to explore how enmity could be translated into empathy by acts of narrative exchange, transforming cycles of violence into radically imaginative moments of welcoming the stranger. The first years of the project (2009–2010) consisted of seminar presentations, academic conferences (philosophical and theological), an internationally streamed poetry festival (Poetries of the Stranger), a music concert (Songs of Sacred Strangeness), and a series of lectures by intellectuals and artists from Noam Chomsky to Anne Carson. The activities were archived on guestbookproject.org and resulted in the publication of two special journal issues and three academic volumes.[6]

Over the years, I was joined by codirectors Sheila Gallagher and Melissa Fitzpatrick as we embarked on a decade-long process of expanding Guestbook beyond an academic program to embrace an international outreach of partnerships on five continents under the umbrella title "Exchanging Stories Changing Histories." This was to become our signature tune, comprising a Narrative Hospitality project of digitally recorded encounters where two young people shared their respective stories across a divide and created a third story together. These were edited as short texts and videos and posted on our Guestbook website, serving as a "classroom without walls," freely accessible to peace leaders, schoolteachers, and community activists in diverse educational contexts (see Figures 1a and 1b).

When I was asked once what motivated me to set up Guestbook, I cited the formative philosophies of hospitality learned from my Paris mentors Ricoeur, Levinas, and Derrida;[7] and I then found myself adding the more biographical fact of growing up in Ireland during a thirty-year period of sectarian strife (1960s–1990s), largely resolved in the Good Friday Peace Agreement of April 1998. The following experience of a dramatic narrative encounter between two ex-paramilitary prisoners in Northern Ireland marked me deeply. This is how I described it in an interview:

> In the 1980s, at the height of "the Troubles" in Northern Ireland, I was invited as a young professor of philosophy to come to Derry, a city divided by war, to moderate a workshop between republican and loyalist prisoners. During the workshop, one of the IRA [Irish Republican Army] prisoners told of how one night he was asleep in his

bed when a loyalist gang broke into the house, bound, gagged and blindfolded him, threw him into the boot of a car, and drove him to a barn outside Derry. Strapped to a chair and about to be shot, he asked if he could smoke a last cigarette. His captor consented and offered him one. And as he smoked the cigarette—very slowly—he told the story of how he had become involved in republican violence: how his grandfather had been brutally murdered by the British police force, how his father had been incarcerated and tortured, how his mother had become an alcoholic and suffered a nervous breakdown, how his brother had been knee-capped and maimed for the rest of his life. . . . And he went on until he finished his cigarette. Then he waited for the gun to go off. But it didn't. There was no sound. No movement. He waited for five minutes, ten minutes, fifteen minutes, twenty minutes—Nothing. Eventually, he managed to free himself and looked around. There was nobody there; the barn was empty. He walked home.

When the IRA prisoner finished sharing this in the workshop I was chairing, another man, a Loyalist paramilitary prisoner, stood up at the back of the hall and said, "I was the assassin who gave you that cigarette. And I would have shot you. But I couldn't shoot you because, when I heard your story, I realized it was my story."[8]

Witnessing this exchange, I was deeply struck by how a basic act of narrative imagination could trigger a transfer of empathy between two sworn enemies, leading to a process of unpredictable pardon and peace.

A second Irish story that informed my understanding of Guestbook, from an historical perspective, was that of "chancing your arm." This is a much older narrative, dating back to 1492 when a bloody civil war was raging in Ireland. The then Earl of Kildare, Gearóid Mór FitzGerald, was besieging his archenemy, James Butler, Earl of Ormonde, in Saint Patrick's Cathedral in Dublin. After much time had elapsed, FitzGerald realized that the cycle of violence couldn't go on, that the vicious bloodletting must end. So he asked Butler to carve open a hole in the door and said: "I'm going to remove my armor and stretch my hand through the gap—you can shake it or cut it off. Cut it off and the war continues, shake it and war ends." Fitzgerald "chanced his arm," as the saying goes. Butler shook his hand and there was peace.[9]

These two stories, drawn from the history of my native war-torn Ireland, tell of transformative acts of translation from hostility to hospitality: acts where enemies became allies, strangers became guests. Explaining ways to reappropriate these stories for our time was a modest effort to

Figures 1a and 1b. Guestbook Project

respond to the basic hermeneutic question: "Where do you speak from?" (*d'où parlez-vous?*).[10]

Guestbook now operates as an international nonprofit, devoted to fostering peace stories through the work of empathic imagination, straddling divides of religion, class, power, and culture in places as far afield as Europe, Asia, Africa, the United States, and the Middle East. While our first Guestbook experiment in hospitality began with a video made by two young students in Derry/Londonderry—one Protestant, one Catholic—switching school uniforms and crossing each other's cultural territories, subsequent examples have included young Turks and Armenians sharing forbidden curse words, Israeli and Palestinian students exchanging symbols (the hijab and Star of David), Congolese and Rwandan refugees confiding traumas, Bangalore Muslims and Hindus crossing rituals, Korean and Japanese youths trading memories of historic conflict, and Syrian immigrants and Greek hosts recounting stories of exodus and welcome.

Each of these exchanges involved crossing borders of heart and mind where young people in divided communities dared to remake history by imagining alternative stories.[11] The young storytellers opted to give a future to the past by translating deep legacies of transgenerational hurt into narrative forms of healing. In short, the goal of Guestbook was to empower young people to "chance their arms"—making bold leaps of imagination toward impossible possibilities of peace.

Twinsome Minds: Crossing Narratives of a Divided History

A second application of narrative hospitality I wish to mention is the Twinsome Minds project: a retelling of Ireland's 1916 rebellion as an act of "double remembrance." This project took the form of a multimedia performance, codirected with artist Sheila Gallagher, which dramatized "double stories" from both sides of the political divide: namely, those who fought in opposing uniforms in the Dublin Easter Rising (April 1916) and in the Battle of the Somme (July 1916).

Complex questions of memory and forgetting confronted us from the outset. Our anecdotes and images sought to brush history against the grain in order to revisit hidden secrets, sufferings, and paradoxes. Genuine remembrance, we tried to show, goes beneath the Grand Narratives of Official History to identify neglected *micronarratives*—stories that turn "backward memory" (bound by repetition compulsion) into "forward memory" (alert to unfulfilled possibilities of the past). We sought to deploy a narrative working through of historical trauma with a view to turning "melancholy into mourning."[12] Each generation, we argued, had to pay its "debt to the dead" before history could be remade. And such remaking required a hospitality of narrative imagination.

The basic thesis of Twinsome Minds was that 1916 was both a great rising and a great sundering—between Ireland and Britain, North and South, nationalism and unionism. There were two ways of reliving that split: either as recurring division, acted out generation after generation, or as an opportunity to host opposing memories in an act of narrative exchange. Such hospitality involved retrieving forgotten tales of both sides—two nations, two places, two persons, two parts of ourselves—and translating those buried conflicts into novel modes of imagining. We sought to show that 1916 was a revolution of mind as well as might. It was as much about cultural imagination as about military insurrection.

The 2016 centenary of the Dublin Rising entailed many military commemorations which ignored the fact that half of the 1916 leaders were poets and that the revolutionary generation that gave birth to the Rising teemed with artists and intellectuals, painters and playwrights, writers and storytellers. So Twinsome Minds suggested that it was time to go beyond martial gun salutes and try to recover, in Yeats's words, "an Ireland the poets had imagined."

Nationalist-militarist memory, British or Irish, had always tended to downplay just how complex 1916 was—particularly for those who lived it. After all, the same year that saw almost 500 die in the Dublin Rising of Easter Week saw 3,500 Irish die at the Battle of the Somme in a single day. Some of the dead in both battles were brothers. This was a time of massive questioning and confusion, and it didn't seem right to remember one half of Ireland's family without remembering the other—especially if one recalled that the 1916 leaders themselves proclaimed an Ireland where "all the children be cherished equally." This meant remembering both the Irish Volunteers who fought against Britain and the Royal Irish Fusiliers who fought with Britain. It meant honoring both the Easter lily symbolizing those who perished in Dublin and the red poppy symbolizing those who died in Flanders. It meant acknowledging what the Irish writer, Sean O'Faolain, called the "Siamese duality of mind" that epitomized Irish-British history.

Irish imagination has always been at its best, James Joyce said, when moving between two "twinsome" minds—that is, when having "two thinks at a time"—and then being open to a third. The Irish are most creative when following a logic of both/and, hosting a mix of double fidelities—religious, national, psychological, cultural: doublings that call for new mediations. For Ireland is an island beside an island, part of an archipelago connected by waterways that make all its people "mongrel islanders." "We are what we are, mongrel pure" as Thomas Kinsella said. Or as another poet, Seamus Heaney, added—regarding his own dual upbringing on the Irish border—"two buckets were easier carried than one, I grew up in between." The key was the *between* which summoned what Heaney called a "symbolic reordering of Ireland" open to new possibilities of "Irishness, Britishness, Europeanness, planitariness, creatureliness, whatever . . ."[13]

The philosophy of "twinsome" minds sought to turn polar opposites into fertile openings. It sought to capture a basic hospitality to paradox that, we believed, prompted the Good Friday Agreement of 1998, ultimately sanctioned by both Britain and Ireland: a peace agreement that took the gun out of Irish politics by allowing people to be "Irish or British or both." That 1998 document, like the 1916 Proclamation itself, is still a promissory notes; but we felt it important that our Irish and British contemporaries be invited to make good on such promise rather than settle for stopgap solutions. In 2016 there were still, shockingly, more than eighty

"Peace Walls" separating communities in Northern Ireland along sectarian lines—and almost 80 percent of education remained religiously segregated. War wounds festered south of the border too. And some old tensions reemerged, alas, in the shadow of Brexit.

As a symbolic gesture beyond such divides, Sheila Gallagher and I proposed to perform stories of people who "grew up in between"—tales of crossed identity often eclipsed by Monumental History. The true enemies of commemoration were not, we argued, complexity and confusion but purity and certitude. As Brian Friel reminds us in his play *Translations*, "confusion is not an ignoble condition." Genuine catharsis comes from a crossing of different stories, transforming binary identities into multiple belongings. So we resolved to complicate and pluralize the memory of 1916 with new acts of narrative hospitality.

To this end, we opened our Twinsome Minds performance (see Figures 2a and 2b) with a series of stories featuring split siblings—brothers and sisters caught on opposite sides of the 1916 drama. We recounted, for example, the story of Cyril and William Stevens who ended up in rival uniforms—khaki and green—fighting rival battles. The story of George and William Irving who read two different recruitment posters on the same Fermanagh wall, one inviting enlistment in the British army, the other in the Irish Volunteers, and chose separate camps. The story of Eoin Callaghan and a childhood school friend finding themselves shooting at each other across a Dublin street. And so on. We encountered many such examples from all over Ireland, North and South—families split between dual loyalties, bequeathing historical wounds that called for a therapeutic labor of transgenerational remembering. For repressed wounds scar the psyche and return to haunt one again and again. The central wager of Twinsome Minds was that the traumas of 1916 needed to be reworked into new images and words by artists and thinkers of subsequent generations. It was time for a hospitality of histories.

It is usually in retrospect that we divide historical muddles into fixed Grand Narratives of binary opposition: Irish versus British, northern versus southern, unionist versus republican. It is after the event that the makers of memory impose neat ideologies on what was a big puzzle at the time. What are now celebrated as deliberate military campaigns were often conducted through foggy dew and swirling smoke. In the lust for simplification, many politicians denied the mess of history, their crude militarist memorials masking the perplexity of human action and passion. But if we recall with Benedict Anderson that every nation is an "imagined community," we can begin to reimagine 1916 in more challenging and complex ways. This is why one needs to recollect not only "the terrible

Figures 2a and 2b. Twinsome Minds

beauty" that was born in 1916 (to cite Yeats) but also the still-births, half-births, or almost-births that never saw the light of day. Genuine commemoration means attending not only to what happened, but also to what did not. The past is not just what has passed but what lives on in memory thanks to arrows of futurity that misfired or whose trajectory was interrupted. As Paul Ricoeur reminds us, history is more than what has taken place; it involves "potential" unrealized aspirations still dormant in the past. And this is why it is the founding events of a community that especially require reimagining, at critical moments, in order to unlock unfinished possibilities. Genuine remembrance involves a narrative hospitality that returns not just to moments of military glory but also to dreams forfeited by history. It signals a work of "anticipatory memory."

The questions we explored with our audiences in Twinsome Minds were these: How do we distinguish between good and bad commemoration? How do we differentiate between what Freud called the healing work of "mourning" and the pathology of "melancholy"? Between narratives that incarcerate and narratives that emancipate?[14]

Twinsome Minds set out to retell stories lost across generations, translating trauma into drama, converting pain and confusion into possibilities of poetic hospitality between strangers. Trauma, as Freud noted, refers to "wounds" so deep they cannot be processed at the time and require a later "working through" in images and words—after the event, *nachträglich*. This is what Freud called the "talking cure" and what he described as the origins of art in his reading of the famous *fort/da* scene of little Ernst at play in *Beyond the Pleasure Principle*. In our Twinsome Minds experiment, we endeavored to suggest ways in which the conflicted histories of 1916 (in Dublin and Flanders) might be translated into stories that allowed for catharsis and healing. We sought ways in which ghosts might be converted into ancestors and the phantoms of 1916 revisited, so that living men and women might return—each with its "local habitation and a name." That is what we were attempting to hint at in our digital projections and recitals in collaboration with a host of other contemporary Irish writers and artists. It was an effort to contribute some form of narrative hospitality to the ongoing reimagining of the unfinished events of 1916 and, by extension, other commemorative moments of Irish history (the Battle of the Boyne, the Walls of Derry, the Famine, the War of Independence, the Civil War, the founding of the Republic, and so on). Needless to say, these projects of continuous reimagining are aimed at the participants of such commemorations beyond the single authors and artists who made them. In fact, if we heed Aristotle in *The Poetics*, it is above all the *audiences* of narrated action (*muthos mimesis*) who experience catharsis.

Good commemoration, we concluded, opens a way beyond polarities of either/or toward a more porous culture of both/and: a culture of mutual translation, of two-way hospitality between competing stories. The 1916 centenary offered the citizens of Ireland and Britain an occasion to transcend the clash of binaries—nationalist or unionist, poppy or lily,

Protestant or Catholic—so that the Irish-British archipelago might escape historical cycles of mimetic enmity and evolve into a more transnational constellation (regional, European, global). This, we wagered, might open possibilities for a postnationalist and post-Unionist imaginary transcending the blockages of inherited frontiers—what we called a "Fifth Province of hospitality" that exceeded the four Irish provinces of north, south, east, and west and the four nations of England, Scotland, Ulster, and Wales.[15] We saw it as a finisterre of hope for new pilgrimages of imagination, while recalling the great cultural enlightenment of 1916: a genuinely pluralist project witnessed in the proliferation of pioneering writings in the first quarter of the twentieth century—daring work ranging from the 1916 leaders themselves, Pearse, Connolly, and Griffith (who all edited intellectual journals), to the bold cosmopolitanism announced by James Joyce when he called for the "hibernising of Europe and the Europeanising of Ireland." A state of mind where everyone could say *mundanus sum*: I belong to the world.

This is a mind of multiple translatability sung by Joyce's Anna Livia, bringer of plurabilities, whose music "rendered all animated greatbritish and Irish" things visible in its "glistery gleam darkling adown affluvial flowandflow."[16] "Mememormee, mememormee," Joyce's washerwomen chimed until, retelling history and forgiving the past, they could say: "lave it so." Lave as in *laver*, to wash and heal the wounds of the past; and also to let be. We'll leave it so. For "too much remembrance," as Brian Friel reminds us, "is a form of madness." There are times to reclaim and times to let go. The centenary of 1916 was a time for both: a challenge of narrative hospitality to translate both ways—twinsomely—having at least "two thinks at a time." Remembering and forgetting in good measure to salve the scars of the past. Forgetting what had been too remembered—the triumphal myths—and remembering what had been too forgotten—the promissory notes.

The work of recovery is in between. Every culture needs a healing of history through a hospitality of stories.[17] A constant remaking of narratives. Exchanging stories, changing histories. Reinventing the past again and again.

The Irish Famine Memorial, New York: Hosting Trauma

In my third example of narrative hospitality, I examine the hermeneutic model of "exchanging stories of suffering."[18] I suggest that certain topographical memorials of trauma (and the violent histories behind such trauma) epitomize an ethics of healing. I choose the Irish Hunger Memorial in Battery Park in New York City, an interactive monument designed and installed by Brian Tolle in 2001 to commemorate the Great Irish Famines of the 1840s and the subsequent emigrations to North America.

Commemoration takes shape in both verbal and nonverbal media. It is arguably the physical monument that elicits the most controversy because it is basically static. Its solidity of presence raises particular issues surrounding the myriad meanings and interpretations experienced by viewers over time. At the root of the difficulty of memorialization—a difficulty also surrounding the 9/11 memorial in New York City or the Vietnam War memorial in Washington for example—is the question: What exactly is to be remembered? Will the monument speak to past actions of people, or toward retrieving that past in the light of different interpretations in the present? When commemoration responds to an act of violence or disaster, these key questions become more ethically vexed. The tension at the heart of the matter resides in the possibility of an abuse of memory—namely, not remembering the complex reality of trauma or remembering it in a way that devalues or misconstrues the victims of calamity.[19]

First, a word about the memorial itself (see Figure 3). The Irish Famine installation consists of a stone cottage transplanted from the west coast of Ireland to Battery Park City at the heart of downtown New York, not far from where the Twin Towers once stood. The memorial does not attempt a nostalgic retrieval of a quaint Irish past—so often invoked by picture postcard versions of the traditional thatched cottage. On the contrary, it seeks to reimagine the famine past in its present condition of destitution and ruin. As such, Brian Tolle's installation might best be described as a hybrid construct which serves as both a commemoration of the Irish famine of the nineteenth century and a site-specific art installation in metropolitan New York in the third millennium marking the ongoing tragedy of world hunger. This double fidelity to separate times, spaces, and agendas, provokes a sense of disorientation that prevents the act of memory regressing to some kind of sentimental fixation with the past (what Ricoeur calls "blocked memory").[20] By the same token it also prevents the exhibit from serving as an exotic curiosity of tourist voyeurism in the present. By breaking open the temporality of history it performs a narrative hospitality to possible futures prefigured by the past.

This is a famine memorial with a difference. Whereas most conventional commemorations of the Famine featured "people without land" (usually leaving on ships from Ireland or arriving off ships in the Americas), we are confronted here with an uncanny experience of "land without people." Though the installation is located at the very heart of one of the world's most populous cities, there are no humans featured. As such it recalls the

Figure 3. Irish Famine Memorial, New York City

"deserted village" of Slievemore in Achill Island, County Mayo, which was the artist's primary source of inspiration for the work: a haunting depopulated row of abandoned stone huts facing out toward the Atlantic. And it is reminiscent, in its way, of other monuments of ruin and abandonment—for example, the bare walls of Machu Picchu in Peru or the floating hulk of the *Marie Celeste*. It is a far cry in any case from the idealized portraits of rural Irish cottages by romantic landscape painters such as Paul Henry or James O'Connor.

Tolle's installation resists mystification by presenting us with a disturbing sense of spatial "thereness" mixed with a sense of temporal "nowness." As we enter the site, we are confronted with a fieldstone cottage, transplanted stone by stone from Ireland, and reconstructed on a quarter-acre of soil in New York City. But it is impossible to feel at home here. This could never be a dwelling for us, contemporary visitors to the cottage. The most obvious reason for this sense of homelessness is, no doubt, the memorial's location at the core of a bustling metropolitan cityscape where it is clearly *out of place*—dislocated literally and symbolically. And the fact that the cottage and surrounding potato drills are themselves planted on a suspended limestone and concrete base doubly confirms one's sense of uncanny *not belonging*.[21] This sentiment of spatial disorientation provokes us, in turn, to reflect on the paradox that our sense of placement in the world often presupposes an acute sense of loss and displacement, as when the Irish Captain McMorris asks "What ish my nation?" in Shakespeare's *Henry* V—his question betraying the fact that he is preoccupied with his national identity precisely because he has *forfeited* it (he is speaking in the English language and wearing an English uniform). Likewise, it has been noted by Irish critics such as Declan Kiberd, Roy Foster, and Luke Gibbons that Irish tradition is in many respects an *invention* of modernity.[22] Just as our sense of the past is almost always configured by our present historical consciousness.[23]

Like Twinsome Minds, Tolle's installation is an invitation to "mourning" (acknowledging that the lost object is lost) rather than "melancholy" (refusing to let go of the lost object by obsessively fixating on it).[24] Soliciting visitors' involvement with the site as part of an ongoing drama of symbolic reinvention, Tolle ensures that the work remains in perpetual progress, intertextually incomplete by definition. The fact that new readings, stories, and reactions are regularly included by Tolle on both the soundtrack of voices, which visitors hear as they traverse the underground tunnel, and the visual inscriptions on the glass panels, are powerful tokens of an active process of narration.[25] The interactive work hosts a multiplicity of competing interpretations, reminding each of us—as guest/participant/visitor/reader—that the most important thing is one's *response* to the invitation.

By deterritorializing the stone cottage from rural Ireland and reterritorializing it amidst the urban bustle of New York, Tolle is reminding us that the place of trauma is always haunted by a no-place of mourning. Such mourning calls for a letting go of the literal landscape of the past in order to open it to new possibilities of imagination. A move from the fetishism of home to the bewilderment of homelessness. And in this we could say that the artist is conjuring up the emancipatory potential of the famous "Fifth Province" in Ireland, mentioned earlier, alongside the other official four provinces—Munster, Ulster, Leinster, and Connaught. As it happens, the Irish word for province is *coiced*, meaning a fifth. So where, one might ask, does the Fifth Province exist, since there are only four existing geographical places? The legendary answer is that it symbolizes a placeless place, a space of detachment rather than attachment, a disposition rather than a position. From the earliest Irish mythologies, this Fifth Province signaled an imaginary site of hospitality offering insights of peace, wisdom and healing to the otherwise warring parts of Ireland.[26] Tolle's memorial might be said to remind us that all our lives—whether we are Irish or non-Irish, native or stranger, survivor or victim—are always haunted by an irretrievable sense of absence and loss, ghosted by a longing for some "irrecoverable elsewhere."[27] A sense of uncanny homelessness.

Tolle attests to the Fifth Province by ensuring that his installation remains a site of hermeneutic hospitality—an interactive multimedia play of diverse perspectives. The hold of a single metanarrative is liberated into a polyphony of discontinuous and competing readings, as Tolle juxtaposes, in both written and audio commentaries, statistics about the Irish Famine with equally perturbing information about other devastating famines throughout history and world hunger generally. He mixes snatches of history and politics with snippets of story, song, and poetry from Ireland and elsewhere. And so doing, he hosts a remarkable variety of vernacular and postmodern art styles—Naturalism, Folk Craft, Conceptual Art, Hyperrealism, Landscape Architecture, Theme Sculpture, Pop Art, and Earth Art. Moreover, the fact that the installation can grow and mutate, thanks to the use of climactically sensitive organic materials and to the deployment of flexible, alterable texts (silkscreened onto strips of clear Plexiglas), illustrates Tolle's conviction that historical memorials are themselves subject to change according to the addition of new and alternative perspectives.[28]

The transatlantic exchange between Mayo and New York—between abandoned stone cottage and postmodern concrete megapolis—invites a response of profound questioning and curiosity in most visitors. It reminds us that if, on entering the site, we pass *from action to text* we return *from text to action* as soon as we exit. Poetic transplantation solicits a hospitality of everyday memory in the real world around us, namely third-millennium Manhattan.

Finally, we might mention that if Tolle's memorial is an "intertext" in so far as it brings together diverse narratives of history and geography, it also functions "countertextually" by mirroring a number of other monuments in the immediate or not so immediate environment: most notably, Ellis Island and the Statue of Liberty visible to the south of the waterfront Memorial—both symbols of aspiration for so many emigrants over the centuries. But it also interfaces with the trauma of the burning Twin Towers themselves, in whose shadow in lower Manhattan the memorial was originally constructed and in whose ruined wake it now stands. And one might add its referencing of other Irish Famine memorials in Boston and Quebec and different emigrant ports of North America, so different and so similar; or monuments to non-Irish historical traumas from the Holocaust to Vietnam—in particular the Museum of Jewish Heritage, a Living Memorial to the Shoah also housed in Battery Park City, or Maya Lin's famous Vietnam Veterans Memorial in Washington.[29] It is just such a work of healing hospitality that memorials like the Battery Park City Famine installation can solicit, reminding us that hospitality is an ongoing process of commemorative commiseration.[30] All strangers are welcome.

In sum, Tolle's installation serves, I submit, as a therapeutic exchange of memories between people of differing identities—Irish, American and non-American,(Asian, African, Middle Eastern, Hispanic, etc.). It also invites an exchange between places - home and abroad, between the Old World and New, between Achill Island and Manhattan Island. And of course, to move from geography back to history, it involves an exchange—in both directions—between past and present. By refusing to either naturalize or aestheticize memory, Tolle keeps open a critical "gap" that prevents history from collapsing into the past. His memorial resists reification by hosting uncanny tensions between now and then, transiting back and forth between the everyday reality of New York life today and the minds of those immigrants who left their home behind well over a century before. It is in this homeless "between" that contemporary guests to the site may experience a genuine hospitality of memory.

Appendix: Ethics, Narrative, and Memory

So how might we relate such commemorations to a specifically *ethical* paradigm of hospitality?

As we saw at the outset of this chapter, Ricoeur suggests that an exchange of memories can provide an ethic of hospitality that involves "taking responsibility for the story of the other, through the life narratives which concern the other."[31] With respect to the three examples we looked at—Guestbook, Twinsome Minds, and the Famine Memorial—this takes the form of an exchange between different people's histories such that we practice an "art of transference" allowing us to welcome the story of the other, the stranger, the victim, the forgotten one. In "Reflections for a new Ethos for Europe," Ricoeur proposes an ethic of flexibility that resists the fixation of an historical event in dogma by showing how each event can be told in different ways by different narrators in different generations. Not that everything becomes relative and arbitrary. On the contrary, acts of trauma and suffering call out for justice, and one way of achieving this is to invite empathy with strangers and adversaries by hosting a plurality of narrative perspectives. The resulting overlap may lead to what Gadamer calls a "fusion of horizons" where diverse horizons of consciousness seek common ground, a reciprocal transfer between opposite minds.[32] "The identity of a group, culture, people, or nation is not that of an immutable substance," writes Ricoeur, "nor that of a fixed structure, but that, rather, of a recounted story." A hermeneutic exchange of stories effectively resists a rigid conception of identity that blocks the process of narrativity—namely, "the possibility of revising every story which has been handed down and of carving out a place for several stories directed towards the same past."[33]

Such an ethical principle of plurality respects the singularity of events through various acts of remembering. It might even be said to increase our appreciation of singularity, especially if the event narrated is foreign to us in time, space, or cultural provenance. *"Recounting differently* is not inimical to a certain historical reverence to the extent that the inexhaustible richness of the event is honored by the diversity of stories which are made of it, and by the competition to which that diversity gives rise."[34] And Ricoeur recalls here the critical point that our ability to recount canonical events of our national history in multiple ways is reinforced by an exchange of memories between different groups within the nation, or between the nation and foreign nations. As our three examples have suggested, the ability to exchange has as touchstone the will to share symbolically and respectfully in the commemoration of the founding events of minority ethnic and religious cultures within one's own nation-state, as well as the founding events of *other* cultures beyond one's nation-state.[35] This point applies as much to events of pain and trauma (commemorated in war or famine memorials) as to events of triumph and glory (the French or American Revolutions), always remembering that one community's victory can be another's calamity. The question of power—who owns history?—calls for constant ethical discernment.

Another aspect of the hospitality of memories is the transfiguring of the past. This involves a creative retrieval of the betrayed promises of history, so that we may respond to our "debt to the dead" and endeavor to give them voice. The goal of memorialization is, on this count, to try to remember history in *better* ways, ethically and poetically. For a crucial aspect of reinterpreting transmitted traditions is, as noted, the task of discerning past promises that have not been honored, possibilities of history that have not yet been realized, remaining for all intents and purposes, "uncompleted projects."[36] In other words, the unactualized *potentials* of history may well signal the richest part of a tradition; and the emancipation of "this unfulfilled future of the past is the major benefit that we can expect from the crossing of memories and the exchange of narratives."[37] Again, it is especially the founding events of a community—traumatic or dramatic—that need to be reread in this critical manner in order to unlock the potencies and expectancies that the subsequent unfolding of history has repressed, forgotten, or travestied. This is why any genuine memorial entails a retrieval of seminal moments of suffering or hope, original events (and responses to those events) all too often occluded by Official History. And it is also why good commemoration is, in Ricoeur's terms, an act of bringing lost moments back to life in the now.[38]

A final moment in the hospitality of memory is forgiveness. If empathy toward others is a pivotal process in the ethics of remembrance, there is often something *more* required—something that entails moving beyond narrative imagination to pardon. In short, an ethical exchange of past wounds demands more than sympathy and duty (though these are essential for any kind of justice); it may also call for a "shattering of the debt." Here the order of just reciprocity can be supplemented, though never replaced, by that of "charity and gift." Such forgiveness, if it occurs, demands huge patience—an enduring practice of mourning and letting go. But it is not a forgetful forgiveness. Amnesty can never be based on amnesia; it remembers our indebtedness to the dead while at the same time introducing something else—namely, hospitality to the shadows of the past sometimes difficult almost to the point of impossibility, but all the more important for that. One thinks of Brandt kneeling at Warsaw, Havel's apology to the Sudeten Germans, Hume's dialogue with the IRA, Sadat's visit to Jerusalem, Hillesum's refusal to hate her hateful persecutors: all moments where an ethics of justice was touched by a poetics of pardon. But, I repeat: one does not replace the other—both justice *and* pardon are important in the hosting of past trauma. As Ricoeur reminds us: "To the degree that charity exceeds justice we must guard against substituting it for justice. Charity remains a surplus; this surplus of compassion and tenderness is capable of giving the exchange of memories its profound motivation, its daring, and its momentum."[39]

It is worth reiterating, in conclusion, that memorials located in places removed from the original trauma—for example, the Holocaust or Irish Famine or Armenian Genocide memorials in New York—can serve the purpose of soliciting empathy not only from the adherents (victims, survivors, descendants) of the particular national events, but from all visitors to the site—regardless of nationality or culture. In short, you don't have to be Jewish, Irish, or Armenian to engage in these respective works of memorialization. And this is where a poetics of narrative hospitality may complement a politics of historical judgment. For when we undertake to visit memorials dedicated to other peoples and communities (not our own), we are suddenly, potentially, all famine victims, all Holocaust sufferers, all casualties of the Armenian genocide or Vietnam War—at least perhaps for an imaginative, fleeting moment.[40]

3

Confessional Hospitality
Translating across Faith Cultures

In Chapter 1, I cited Ricoeur's invocation of "eucharistic hospitality" as a possible corollary of linguistic hospitality. In a concluding note to "Reflections on a New Ethos for Europe," Ricoeur revisits the idea of "interconfessional hospitality," first sketched out in *On Translation*.

Referring specifically to what he calls "Christian denominations" (including his own liberal Protestant faith), Ricoeur suggests they have a crucial ecumenical role to play in the threefold work of crossed narration, mutual translation, and compassion. Ricoeur relates this responsibility for interfaith dialogue to the Gospel message of loving one's neighbors. It is a call to compassion that motivates the translation from one cultural/ecclesial language to another. Ricoeur, a French Protestant, is particularly sensitive to the catastrophic history of the "wars of religion" that ravaged the European continent for centuries. These conflicts included violence waged between the Western churches—Catholic, Lutheran, Calvinist, Methodist—as well as between Western Christendom and the Eastern Churches, and between Christianity tout court and the Islamic religion. (Not to mention the battles with non-Abrahamic religions on other continents.)

One prerequisite for engaging in ecumenical dialogue is the renunciation of power. This power may be understood as a legacy of the Roman Empire or as the hegemonic politics exercised by centralized nation-states since the eighteenth and nineteenth centuries. Within the European arena particularly, Ricoeur calls for the replacement of one kind of "theological politics" with another—without power. It is necessary for Christian denominations to break with a theology that justified domination in top-down relations—Christendom, colonialism, and nation-state religions—in order to embrace a different theology "where the ecclesia, asserting itself as a place of mutual aid with a view to salvation, would truly become a model of fraternity for all the other institutions."[1] But secular society will not heed the Christian narrative of peace and hospitality until and unless Christianity does its own work of "interdenominational exchange" regarding the healing and forgiving of past wounds.[2] When it comes to religion, hospitality begins at home—between religions. Confessional hospitality exists in the plural. Or as Ricoeur puts it: "It is primarily with regard to each other that the Christian communities must exercise mutual forgiveness in order to 'shatter the debt' inherited from a long history of persecution, inquisition, repression, acts of violence which were perpetrated by some communities against others or by all of the communities against non-Christians and non-believers."[3]

Sometimes, as noted in the last chapter, the hospitality of pardon requires us to supplement the laws of justice with something "extra"—the grace of "charity and gift."[4] Christian forgiveness of past sins does not mean forgetting; to the contrary, it means remembering in the right way in order to forgive the unforgivable. Relating this to our prior discussion of translating between host and guest languages, we recall this central claim: "To communicate at the level where we have conducted the work of translation, with its art of transference and its ethics of linguistic hospitality, calls for this further step: that of taking responsibility . . . for the story of the other, through the life narratives which concern that other."[5]

Another timely contribution to the discussion of confessional hospitality is the debate on the role of religion and secularity conducted by Jürgen Habermas with Jacques Derrida and Joseph Ratzinger. Interestingly, all agree with Ricoeur on the central need for "hospitality" in our modern political discourse.[6] While they speak from different perspectives—Habermas, secular; Derrida, Messianic: Ratzinger, Catholic—they all concur that hospitality offers a radical alternative, however complicated, to the infamous friend-enemy opposition made current by Samuel Huntington after 9/11. (I refer to the schismatic split invoked by political zealots on both sides of the "axis of evil").[7] Faced with Huntington's claim that "we only know who we are . . . when we know whom we are against,"[8] the proponents of an ethics of hospitality rejoin that the stranger is precisely the one who reminds us—not as foe but as host—that the self is never an isolated identity but a guest faced with its host. Thus, at a practical level, the ethics of hospitality resists the apocalyptic dualism of pure/impure famously invoked by crusaders like Hitler and Stalin, Bush and Bin Laden, Trump and Kim Jong-un, or countless ideological zealots throughout the ages. The ethics of hospitality opposes such Gnostic divides where God is on my side and the Stranger is the devil in disguise.

While Habermas proposes a model of hospitality to overcome the state of nature in the name of reciprocal respect between equal members of a civic secular society, Derrida (true to form) identifies the "messianic" structure of hospitality as an affirmation of the "impossible." The difference is important. To clarify: Habermas seeks to sublimate the religious roots of hospitality into a "discourse ethics" of rational norms and universalizable laws.[9] He maintains that religion, defined as a "comprehensive world-view which claims to structure a life in its entirety," is legitimate if it can be translated into the language of secular culture where it can be evaluated and negotiated—that is, rationally discussed. Religion is eligible in modern democracy, accordingly, on condition that it is "sublated" into reasonable ethical discourse. Habermas concedes that political liberalism goes too far if it refuses to allow religious believers to participate in the public sphere. Religious identity, he admits, is not clandestine and is not something utterly alien to, or incompatible with, sociopolitical-normative existence.[10] The liberal state, he counsels, "must not transform the requisite *institutional* separation of religion and politics into an undue *mental* and *psychological* burden for those of its citizens who follow a faith."[11] It is here that Habermas makes his most decisive move. He introduces what he calls an "institutional translation proviso." This allows religious believers—who accept that only "secular reasons count beyond the institutional threshold"—to express their beliefs in a specifically confessional language *if* they can find "secular translations for them."[12] On this condition, religious convictions (which Habermas describes as "private reasons") may indeed be admitted to the public sphere for functional or discursive purposes. The translation proviso aims to avoid an unbridgeable chasm between private religious faith and public political reason, and it operates, I repeat, on the assumption that persuasions of faith remain open to possibilities of further translation and assimilation into the language of reason. Once confessional beliefs are thus admitted, it remains the task of a democratic liberal society to encourage such "religious consciousness (to) become reflective and secular consciousness transcending its limitation in a mutual learning process."[13] The concessions are, in principle, reciprocal.

But while this may seem like a fair carving up of responsibilities, it is in fact unequal. For what appears like bilateral mobility between faith and reason is really, deep down, a one-way street. Close reading shows that for Habermas the goal of such "mutual learning" is ultimately for religion to become more translatable into the rational normative pedagogy process and not, as would be fair, for secular reason to simultaneously "transcend *its* limitations" (the other half of the bargain). The secular pedagogy process is surely desirable, but it should, I submit, work equally and in *both* directions at once. Secularity should be modest enough to acknowledge the possibility of a certain untranslatable remainder, a *surplus* of meaning that bypasses the limits of normative rationality. But Habermas does not press this point. Rather, it seems the ultimate goal of a democratic society for him is to integrate a plurality of faith cultures into an institutionalized discourse of clearly shared and accessible deliberation.[14] And here—in dialogue with Ratzinger—he cites Judeo-Christianity as an ideal candidate for such progressive pedagogy, since many of its religious legacies have already been translated into founding principles of Western democratic enlightenment. Christian theology and philosophy have, it seems, proved their mettle over history. Habermas is clear on this point:

> For the normative self-understanding of modernity, Christianity has functioned as more than just a precursor or a catalyst. Universalistic egalitarianism, from which sprang ideals of freedom and a collective life in solidarity, the autonomous conduct of life and emancipation, the individual morality of conscience, human rights and democracy, is the direct legacy of the Judaic ethic of justice and the Christian ethic of love.[15]

He concludes, "This legacy . . . has been the object of a continual critical reappropriation and reinterpretation. Up to this very day there is no alternative to it. And in light of current challenges of a postnational constellation, we must draw sustenance now, as in the past, from this substance. Everything else is idle postmodern talk."[16] By "idle postmodern talk," one presumes Habermas is referring not only to posthumanist relativism but to New Age spiritualism and eclecticism.

Several difficulties arise here. First, how hospitable is Habermas's model of secular hospitality to religion? In such a rationalizing scenario, how does one react to the radically new and surprising? To the mystical and mysterious? To the numinous and transcendent? How do we accommodate the stranger without trying to translate him/her into the accredited terms of Western reason? How do we respond to what Derrida and Benjamin call the "messianic"? In short, it would appear that for Habermas the final aim of societal reason is to "completely assimilate, translate, rework and sublate all desirable religious content."[17] But how then respect belief in divinity as a transcendent Other which reveals itself? A Stranger who solicits and calls, arrives and invites, revealing signs "which surpass our understanding?" How, in such a coopting secular scenario, do we host the visitor from outside our "rational" home, opening our gates to unpredictable epiphanies never dreamt of in the philosophies of Horatio or Habermas? How, in a word, is secular reason to account for that extra of alterity which—precisely as foreign, sacred, messianic—always remains partially unassimilable and inaccessible to our normative and normalizing grasp? Or to speak in terms of political migration, can aliens only become guests as *Gastarbeiter*, to be tolerated in so far as they surrender their irreducible singularity to the sovereign master of the house? It is not sure in fact that Habermas's "pubic sphere of reason" can really welcome radical strangers. He does not seem to have a host language sufficiently vigilant of its own limits to respect what Benjamin calls the "untranslatable kernel" at the heart of every guest language—namely, that irreducible transcendence which puts the host into question, shatters one's self-security and exposes one to the incoming Other.[18] In a word, Habermas's ethic of hospitality would seem, at the limit, to be too conditioned and conditional, not sufficiently open to the "messianic" perspective of Derrida, Benjamin, and Levinas. Melissa Fitzpatrick will be exploring this question of hosting untranslatable alterity in Part II.

Further problems are apparent, I suspect, in Habermas's omission of any reference to Islam and other religions. It is not easy, in fact, to square Habermas's telos of "universal rational translatability" with real interconfessional hospitality. For how can one neglect the responsibility of any civic society to host religions *other* than the European tradition of Judeo-Christian humanism? What of the religions of the East or, closer to home, of Muslim believers both inside and outside the borders of Western society? Are only those believers to be accepted whose translation from faith into reason has "already occurred . . . in the political public sphere itself"?[19] On this score, I think that Lovisa Bergdahl is right to say that Habermas has a Eurocentric notion of religious pluralism, one that privileges familiar religious neighbors over unfamiliar strangers. By contrast, the true task of translation, as Bergdahl reminds us, is to acknowledge the *double* call of the stranger: translate me/do not translate me! For the real challenge is to respect "the unfathomable, the mysterious and the poetic superfluity of meanings" while making as much shared sense as we can.[20] In short, the biggest temptation for the translator—in practicing an ethics of hospitality between faiths—is to conserve the status quo of one's host culture without allowing oneself to be genuinely transformed by the foreignness of the guest.[21] When it comes to religion, to yield to such temptation is to close the door to the confessional stranger. It is to decline the wager of interconfessional hospitality.

Finally, one might object that Habermas's hospitality of enlightenment always assumes the role of host, never that of guest. It never seems to consider what it might mean for European secular reason to be a guest translated and hosted by the culture of religious strangers? After all, the Abrahamic religions of the Book are all informed, as we noted, by stories of strangers from afar being hosted by the given religion of the time—whether it is the three strangers at Mamre, the Shulamite woman in the Song of Songs, Ruth the Moabite, the three wise Kings, the Syro-Phoenician woman, or countless aliens, foreigners, and migrants celebrated throughout the Judeo-Christian scriptures. And mystical Islam is well known for its hospitality to the outsider, made legendary in Rumi's poetics of the divine stranger as "uninvited guest." Not to mention the daring manner in which Judaism, Christianity, and Islam all invited the great thinkers of Athens—representing the genius of Greek philosophy—into the three faiths of Jerusalem. Think of Maimonides, Augustine, Aquinas, Avicenna, Averroes. By seeing hospitality as the prerogative of Western secular rational hosts—unilaterally offered to faith-bearing guests (*hostes*)—the Habermasian humanist project, however laudable in its pursuit of liberty, fraternity, and equality, falls short when it comes to hospitality, properly understood as a *reversible* relation between host and guest.

True hospitality is a two-way street, where we are all others to each other, and always strangers to ourselves.[22]

4

Carnal Hospitality
Gesturing beyond Apartheid

An ethics of hospitality, I hope to have shown, involves empathizing with others though the exchange of stories, memories, and faiths—the aim being to work through the wounds of history and open a space for charity and gift.[1] This, we saw, involved moving beyond a mere reciprocity of exchange to a difficult, almost impossible, order of grace—a leap which transcends the strict laws of justice in the name of something "more": namely, forgiving the enemy and shattering the debt. Here law is supplemented by love, and in this step toward a higher poetics of pardon there comes a point where narrative exchange—of histories, traditions, confessions, testimonies—often needs to be supplemented by an exchange of physical gestures, a point where narrative hospitality calls for carnal hospitality: where the textual solicits the tactile, where word gives way to touch.

Civilization, Marina Warner argues, begins with the handshake.[2] Instead of reaching for a sword, one offers one's hand. The fist unfurls into an open palm. The *hostis*-enemy becomes the *hostis*-friend. We read of such primal scenes of carnal hospitality from the origins of time. Recall Homer's *Iliad* where the archrivals Glaucon and Adeimantus cast away spears of enmity to embrace each other rather than repeat old cycles of revenge, or the primal scenes in the Bible where Abraham and Sarah offer three strangers bread made from their own hands, or where Jacob body wrestles with the angel until he reveals the name of Israel, or where Christ heals strangers with the touch of a hand? And this power of touch is a recurring story in some of the great handshakes of our own time: moments of physical encounter that transform wounds of hostility into "marvels of hospitality"—recall Mandela and De Klerk, McGuinness and Paisley, Rabin and Arafat, Gandhi and Mountbatten. One wages war or chances one's arm.[3]

Carnal hospitality operates through the five senses—but it is arguably in touch that our most basic exposure to the other occurs.[4] Phenomenology gives a hint of this when Husserl shows in *Ideas 2* how empathy works through the "double sensation" of touch—a phenomenon of reversibility where touching is also a being touched. This simple insight into the active-passive experience of a hand touching and being touched has been developed by thinkers such as Merleau-Ponty with his phenomenology of the body-subject and by Kristeva with her semiotic notion of *reliance*. But the basic idea was already announced by Aristotle in the first work of human psychology, the *De Anima*, when he declared that "touch is the most philosophical" of the senses. What he meant by this startling claim is that touch is the most "universal" sense since it is operative in all our sensing: light touches the eye, salt the tongue, sound the ear, and so on. The only parts of a human person that have no tactile feelings are our hair and nails. (You can cut both without pain.) The tactile-tangible body is the vulnerable body, exposing us to otherness—to the experience of what is different from ourselves. "Touch discerns differences," says Aristotle, using the Greek verb *krinein*: to discriminate carnally between distinct things. The body feels what is hotter and colder than itself. We feel what is *other* than ourselves. We host the strangeness that interrupts our being, as Melissa Fitzpatrick reminds us in Part II. Familiarity breeds indifference. Egotism is sense-less. The sense of touch, in short, is what exposes us to risk and adventure, to novelty and natality—to what is happening when we touch and are touched by others (human, mineral, animal, or divine). That is why Aristotle suggests that the smooth-skinned person is the most sensible because the most sensitive. Virtue comes from reciprocal feeling, empathy, attention, whereas vices like gluttony and wantonness come from the betrayal of sensitivity: turning our natural propensity for two-way touching into one-way grasping (namely, the imposition of *my* feelings on others without being receptive to *their*s in return). The hand and mouth are two of the most sensitive organs of the human body. The bare palm and naked lips signal exposure. This is why the kiss and handshake are primal symbols of hospitality.

But handshakes are facile if we do not appreciate the risks involved. Peace is empty (mere tokenism) if the hands that meet are not truly in touch. If there is not tact in the contact. By way of illustrating the radicality of hand to hand contact in genuine gestures of hospitality and healing, I offer here the example of Pumla Gobodo-Madikizela, a pioneering South

African scholar and peace activist who served on the Truth and Reconciliation Movement in the 1990s and with whom I had the honor of conversing during a visit to Stellenbosch in May 2017. One story she recounted exemplified for me the principle of carnal hospitality—the "double sensation" of touching and being touched—even in the most inhospitable of circumstances.[5]

Here is the story: Pumla decided, during a sensitive moment in the reconciliation process, to meet Eugene de Kock, a brutal apartheid executioner known popularly as "Prime Evil," then in prison. She bore no illusions: "De Kock had not just given apartheid's murderous evil a name. He had become that evil."[6] Pumla was prompted to meet with this notorious assassin after she heard a widow of one of his victims express a willingness to forgive him after witnessing his testimony to the Truth and Reconciliation Commission (TRC) in September 1997. "I would like to hold him by the hand," the widow had said, "and show him that there is a future, and that he can still change."[7] Pumla was deeply struck by these words and interpreted the widow's readiness to reach out to her husband's murderer as an astonishing, almost impossible, act of empathy; for the widow was not only shedding tears for the loss of her own executed spouse but for the loss of De Kock's moral humanity. This raised the crucial question: "Was de Kock deserving of the forgiveness shown to him. . . . Was evil intrinsic to de Kock, and forgiveness wasted on him?"[8] Or as Augustine would have it: Was it possible to unbind the agent from the act?[9]

Pumla realized that De Kock's statement of apology at the TRC was a step in the pardoning process, but she was also aware of the asymmetry between an avowal of guilt and the act of forgiving the perpetrator, whose words may have an empty ring to them, "adding insult to injury."[10] However, the power and significance of an apology lay, Pumla believed in its ability "to *perform* and to transcend the apologetic words."[11] The emphasis on embodied "performance" was crucial. Why? Because, as Pumla put it, "empathy is what enables us to recognize another's pain, even in the midst of tragedy, because pain cannot be evil. Empathy deepens our humanity. . . . When perpetrators apologize and experience the pain of remorse, showing contrition, they are *acting as human beings*."[12] During her encounter with De Kock in prison, Pumla was at one point surprised by his tears as he confessed not only his regret at murdering the widow's husband but also his desire to undo the wrong: "I wish there was a way of bringing the (body) back alive. I wish I could say, 'Here (is) your husband.' He confided this, stretching out his arms as if bearing an invisible body, his hands trembling, his mouth quivering, adding "but unfortunately . . . I have to live with it'"[13]

And then the impossible happened—an unthinkable act of carnal transference. Pumla touched his hand. Almost unbeknownst to herself, she found herself reaching out, only to find his hand clenched as a fist, "cold and rigid." Reflecting back on this gesture afterward, she observed: "This made me recoil for a moment and to recast my act of reaching out as something incompatible with the circumstances of an encounter with a person who not too long ago used these same hands, this same voice, to authorize and initiate unspeakable acts of malice against (black) people very much like myself."[14]

This was no cheap grace. If anything, the strange unpredictable moment signaled an event of "impossible hospitality." Pumla's encounter with De Kock left her with a certain guilt at having experienced an instant of empathy, making her wonder if she had not "crossed the moral line from compassion, which allows some measure of distance, to actually identifying with De Kock."[15] The encounter also had an impact on De Kock himself. During one of their later meetings, he confessed: "You know, Pumla, that was my trigger hand you touched."[16] This chilling admission left Pumla with a mixture of feelings. On the one hand, she felt vulnerable, angry, and invaded, while on the other she recognized that De Kock's statement might also carry an underlying subtext: "My action may well have been the first time a black person touched him out of compassion. He had previously met black people only as enemies, across the barrel of a gun. . . . Perhaps de Kock *recognized my touch as a kind of threshold crossing*, a new experience for him."[17] But such liminal crossing was far from evident. Pumla was painfully aware of the contradictions involved in touching the "trigger hand," yet at that moment of carnal exchange she did not withdraw her hand. She made a wager in the impossible possibility of a shared humanity. "His world was a cold world," she realized, "where eyes of death stared accusingly at him, a world littered with corpses and graves. . . . But for all the horrific singularity of his acts, de Kock was a desperate soul seeking to affirm to himself that he was still part of the human universe."[18]

What is so revealing about this "trigger hand" episode is, I think, that it was Pumla's carnal experience of De Kock's remorse that reciprocally triggered her ability to acknowledge his humanity.[19] That momentary gesture of pardon—or grace?—worked, it seems, because both De Kock's remorse and Pumla's empathy were *carnally performed* rather than just *conceptually calculated*. It was less about cognition than recognition, less about making sense than sharing sensibility. "A genuine apology," as Pumla subsequently concluded, "focuses on the feelings of the other rather than on how the one who is apologizing is going to benefit in the end. It seeks to acknowledge full responsibility for the act . . . and must communicate, convey, and *perform* as a 'speech act' that expresses a desire to right the relationship damaged through the action of the apologizer."[20] In short, the act of *double performativity* between Pumla and de Kock embodied a dual acknowledgment of common humanity between self and stranger, forgiver and executioner, peacemaker and criminal. Or as Pumla herself put it, extending her experience to the work of the TRC: "When remorse is triggered in the moment of witnessing . . . the perpetrator recognizes the other as a fellow human being." At the same time, the victim, too, recognizes the face of the perpetrator not as that of a "monster" who committed terrible deeds, but as a face with enough humanity to feel remorse.[21] Such moments of forgiveness, to the extent that they are possible, lie in the search "not for the things that separate us but for something common among us fellow human beings, the compassion and empathy that bind our human identity."[22]

Commenting on Pumla Gobodo-Madikizela's performance during the TRC, Archbishop Desmond Tutu remarked: "We should all be deeply humbled by what we've heard. . . . Now we've got to turn our backs on this awful past and say: life is for living."[23] "After such knowledge what forgiveness?" asks T. S. Eliot. And we might add, in the spirit of Tutu and Gobodo-Madikizela: "After such forgiveness what knowledge?" For if there *is* knowledge, what kind of knowledge is it? Cognitive or embodied—or both? And what do we do with it? Do we go on remembering, working through wounds, setting the record straight? Or do we also try to forgive and forget? There are handshakes that signal a readiness to recall and others which signal a time to let go. This is a key problem not only for the Truth and Reconciliation Commission in South Africa but also for countless other truth tribunals and memorials in posttraumatic communities throughout the world.

So why, we ask again, the importance of hands? Triggering or calming, acting or suffering, criminal or reconciling? And how might such hand contact convert enemies (*hostes*) into fellow humans? What most strikes me about Pumla's account is her witness to a form of practical wisdom that operates through the body, a discerning sensibility which functions at the level of skin and flesh, nerve endings and sinews, complexion and touch. This is what I have elsewhere called "carnal hermeneutics"—a carnal knowing prior to reflective knowing, a form of tact within contact, of savvy in the original sense of tasting and testing what is apt and right. Whence the etymological lineage of savvy: *savoir/savourer/sapere/sapientia*. It connotes a primal embodied wisdom operating in the three senses of sense—as sensation, orientation, and meaning—that mark every genuine encounter between self and stranger. When this carnal power of savvy is at work, it is not impossible for enemies to be become friends, for strangers to become guests. In short, for hostility to be transformed into hospitality.[24]

But the matter is not always simple. The meaning of handshakes can also be perverted and abused, symbolic gestures degenerating into ceremonial clichés, malevolent contracts, devious strategies, and power ploys. This raises many critical questions. Who has the right to shake hands with whom? Who decides? And to what purpose and with what motives—stated, hidden, or ulterior? What of the steel fist in the silk glove? What of the infamous World War II handshakes of Hitler with Pétain (and Chamberlain), or of Stalin with Ribbentrop? Or more recently, the chilling clasp of Putin with Assad or the triumphal grip of Trump with Xi Jinping? And what of the dismissal of certain immigrant or minority groups (orthodox Jews or Muslims for example) whose religious mores preclude them from shaking hands with certain people in certain circumstances? In such coded circumstances, the ostensibly "universal" gesture of shaking hands can be used as a means of excluding others.[25]

Because of such variables there is, I submit, an ethical responsibility to discern between handshakes—those that express hospitality and those that express the opposite. A hermeneutics of suspicion (regarding masked motivations, interests, and intentions) needs to accompany a hermeneutics of affirmation (regarding genuine acts of peace, pardon, and reconciliation). And what is true of the handshake is equally true of other carnal gestures of hospitable portent. Think of the kiss as act of love or betrayal (e.g., the kiss of traitors or predators where the "double sensation" of touch is replaced by one-way violation). Think of the giving of food as an act of generosity or poison. For every last supper there are examples of treachery and deceit. Events of hospitable feasting can degenerate into tyrannies of force—the Torah tells of Israelites murdered because they refused unclean food, and consumers of contemporary popular culture can cite the massacre of the Stark family in *Game of Thrones*. Carnal eros too can degenerate into harassment or rape. Not all love making is loving. Just as not all "laying on of hands" is healing (viz the cultic practices of Jim Jones, David Koresh, or Charlie Manson). And one might also recall here the psychoanalytic controversies between Freud, Jung, and Reich, where the phenomenon of "transference" became a complex matter of knowing how to move between word and touch. (Words, we know, can be as erotic as touch—as the annals of seduction indicate from Casanova and *Les liaisons dangereuses* to Kierkegaard's *Diary of a Seducer*.) This is why an ethics of hospitality is as much about knowing when *not* to speak as to speak, when *not* to touch as to touch. Sometimes it is wise to remain silent, placing a compassionate hand on a shoulder; other times, it is wiser to suspend direct contact and move to language.

These distinctions are critical and call for a "pedagogy of tact" regarding modalities of contact. Such discriminations require a hermeneutics of hospitality invigilating the line between the verbal and the tactile.[26] There is touch and touch; and always a gap in between for hosts and guests to discern. As we know from phenomenology, there can be touch by contact and touch at a distance. Being in the presence of someone can be deeply "touching" even if one never makes literal contact. A wave of the hand can be a handshake by other means—and no less powerful for that in certain circumstances. As poet Fanny Howe writes, "sometimes the guest must leave the host in order to remain a guest." It is all a matter of carnal hermeneutics in the end—discerning tactfully between touching and not touching, speaking and being silent. A question of choosing the right gesture with the right person at the right time. Here the dialectic between what we might call apo-haptics and kata-haptics mimes the old dialectic between apo-phatics and kata-phatics. We need both. Knowing how to be far and near, absent and present, foreign and familiar in good measure. Otherwise there is no real distinction between host and guest. No separation, no gap, no risk, no wager, no *épreuve de l'étranger.* No otherness to acknowledge and embrace. We always need the space between. Which is why carnal hospitality is always, at root, an ethical task—never a fait accompli.

One is compelled to add that in the time of coronavirus this whole question of touch is given critical urgency. We will return to this in our postscript.

Concluding Remarks

Carnal contact, we noted, can easily turn from hospitality to hostility—and back again. Different cultures have different ways of interpreting the hospitable exchange of vulnerability and welcome. The hand-to-hand clasp can be replaced, for instance, by a raising of arms, a bending of knees or a bowing of heads. And there are varying codes for such exchanges dependent on gender, age, class, and culture. While the handclasp is a signifier of peace in most Western cultures, it is not true of all cultures. In certain martial arts traditions of China, hospitality is marked by a withholding of one's right hand within the palm of one's left, as one bows before a stranger.[27] In parts of Pakistan specific gestures are used to send the message of friendship, given that it is religiously forbidden for a man to touch a woman without an agreed relationship between the two. According to the Islamic traditions of Pakistan and India, there are basically three ways of greeting based on gender, age, and relationship. When a similar-aged man meets a man, or a woman meets a woman, they shake hands followed by a hug, once on either side. When people of the same age but opposite genders meet, they avoid touching each other and just make eye contact, lowering their looks respectfully in addition to uttering the words "*asalam-ulalikum*." And when a younger person meets an older person, he or she bows in respect for the elder so that the latter is able to touch the head of the former, accompanied by a formula of greeting.[28]

Keeping these and other variations of embodied hospitality in mind, we may conclude that while the paradigm of the handshake is not universally normative, in most Indo-European cultures it signaled a vital gesture of trusting the stranger. Such a disarming act is by definition *reciprocal*, though not always *symmetrical*. Any genuine welcome of the stranger acknowledges the stranger's singular otherness. (If anything, one might speak here of a symmetry of asymmetry.) That is precisely why *hostis* can mean either enemy or friend—one never knows beforehand, only after one chances one's arm (or equivalent gesture). Hence the ineluctable character of risk and wager. In sum, the carnal gesture of hospitality does not entail a reduction of guest to host, nor a surrender of guest to host—but a sharing across difference. Any reduction of strangeness to sameness would signal a totalizing assimilation of alterity, just as the reverse would signal invertebrate submission. Hospitality hangs between.

I would concur with Paul Ricoeur, therefore, that true hospitality is not an exchange between same and same (*même* and *même*), but between similar and similar (*semblable* and *semblable*). If hospitality means being "oneself *as* another" this does not mean being identical with the other; it is not fusion or confusion. The preposition *as* here is critical, marking a caesura of difference between self and other. And not just for Ricoeur, but for Merleau-Ponty too where (*pace* Derrida's accusation of haptocentrism in *On Touching*) the "chiasm of flesh" always retains a "diacritical" space (*écart*) between the self touching and the other touched.[29] Merleau-Ponty insists on this spacing-distancing aspect of "diacritical perception" lest bodies reduce strangeness to totalizing possession—as happens in extremis in molestation, rape, torture or the domineering handgrip of tyrants. In such betrayals of hospitality, two-way sensation (receptive to the other's needs, desires, wounds, singularities) is travestied as one-way imposition (a power play insensitive to the other's being). This is why we need an ethics of practical wisdom (*phronesis*) to discriminate between the tacit intentions of every handshake—an ethics inspired by Aristotle's insistence that touch is the most "philosophical" of the senses because it "knows differences" (it discerns, *krinein*). You can see without being seen, hear without being heard, but you cannot touch without being touched. Which is not to deny that we are free to betray touch, as Aristotle concedes in the

Nicomachean Ethics when he describes drunkenness and lust as unethical modes of absorbing otherness to ourselves. One-way sensualism betrays two-way sensibility. That is why an ethics of hospitality means both a leap of trust in the stranger and a constant act of questioning: *What does this handshake mean? Who comes? And how do they come—in war or in peace? As host or guest? As enemy of friend?* Questions asked in word and gesture. With endless vigilance and discernment.

In short, an ethical play of word and flesh is necessary for real hospitality to happen. We need linguistic *and* carnal hosting for wounds to be healed, strangers to be welcomed and peace to take place.

PART II

Hospitality and Moral Psychology
Exploring the Border between Theory and Practice

MELISSA FITZPATRICK

5

Hospitality beyond Borders
The Case of Kant

It is important to begin by noting that this second part of the volume will use hospitality in two distinct albeit related senses: the first, hosting the *stranger* (in the sense of a human other person); and the second, hosting the *strange* (in the sense of novelty, future, surprise, rupture, challenge, wonder, risk—the unpredictable). It seems clear that the latter type of hospitality in some sense conditions the former, since the otherness of the other person involves an infinite capacity for interruption, despite the common ground that can and should be forged through empathy in narrative imagination, as depicted in Part I.

The four chapters that follow will build from the illustrations of translation, empathy, and carnal hospitality preceding them, analyzing the various ways in which these two senses of hospitality are deeply intertwined by probing—through the lens of moral psychology and the phenomenology of alterity—the experience of being host and guest, and asking why we shirk away from hospitality's wager. The conclusion will point toward the classroom as a fundamental space in which the phenomenology of alterity and the hermeneutics of empathy fruitfully converse and converge.

Although Kant's moral project serves as a point of critique in various accounts of ethics, given its hyperrational, universalizable understanding of morality, Kant is without question the most important—indeed, indispensable—modern thinker of hospitality, and central to all of the philosophical debates on hospitality. As a father of the notion of universal human rights, Kant was ahead of his time; his (later) resistance to slavery, imperialism, and general hostility to strangers was unpopular in the eighteenth century.

Whether or not one agrees with the rigid strictures of Kant's categorical imperative, his project crucially emphasizes an incontestable dimension of human existence: the experience of being compelled to consider others before oneself. Or, to put it in the terms of this volume as sketched out in Part I, the wager of hospitality over hostility.[1] Kant deals with this wager at the level of individual moral psychology and notably deals with it in his short treatise, *Toward Perpetual Peace: A Philosophical Project*, which envisions a World Republic and the conditions of its possibility. For Kant, world peace requires a true cessation of hostility—including standing militaries during times of "peace"—which is, above all, guaranteed by a *global* understanding that each and every one of earth's inhabitants has intrinsic dignity by virtue of being free—equal to every other in that freedom. This understanding is notably grounded in what Kant famously calls the "right to hospitality."

This chapter will provide a hermeneutic of Kant's notion of international hospitality as it relates to his phenomenology of respect—experiencing the moral law—and the call to hold space open for the freedom and dignity of the other. My ultimate claim is that hospitality in Kant's world involves welcoming the freedom of others both within and beyond domestic borders (hosting the stranger)—including the unknown and unforeseeable consequences that freedom so construed necessarily entails (hosting the strange). This is to say that acting from duty, out of respect for the other, can be understood as *acting in hospitality*, while acting from inclination, disrespecting the other in the service of oneself, can be understood as *acting in hostility*.

Toward Perpetual Peace

In *Toward Perpetual Peace*, Kant stresses that each society, like a tree trunk, has its own roots (8:344). A society of people is not, therefore, a thing that can be annexed and grafted on to something else, but instead constitutes a dignity unto itself. He highlights the dangerous presumption in then-Europe that states can *marry each other*, denoting, by his account, a new form of industry for making oneself dominant through family alliances and the expansion of land (ibid.). Kant is disturbed by the fact that no legislative authority exists that can prohibit the imperializing forces of one nation on another—interfering with their constitution, and exercising acts of hostility (vicious forms of torture, the employment of assassins, and various forms of dishonesty, e.g., going back on promises, espionage, etc.) that can potentially render mutual trust obsolete during future peace (8:347). A basic level of trust is essential for sociopolitical relations; and Kant is, of course, notorious for his position on every instance of lying being immoral, as it breaks down the basic function of promises, as well as the earnest pursuit of truth—enlightenment—in the world.

With this in mind, Kant uses the language of hospitality in his definitive articles for perpetual peace, emphasizing, "cosmopolitan right shall be limited to conditions of universal hospitality" (8:357). On this, he writes:

> Here as in the preceding articles, it is not a question of philanthropy but of right, so that hospitality (hospitableness) means the right of a foreigner not to be treated with hostility because he has arrived on the land of another. The other can turn him away, if this can be done without destroying him, but as long as he behaves peaceable where he is, he cannot be treated with hostility. What he can claim is not the right to be a guest (for this a special beneficent pact would be required, making him a member of the household for a certain time), but the right to visit; this right, to present oneself for society, belongs to all human beings *by virtue of the right of possession in common of the earth's surface* on which we cannot disperse infinitely but must finally put up with being near one another; but originally no one had more right than another to be on a place on earth. (8:358, emphasis mine)

Thus, the crucial dimensions of hospitality, as Kant construes it, is that it is a right, not a privilege (it is one's duty to grant hospitality to another insofar as the other is a human being, not an act of charity); and that it is a negative right in the sense that a foreigner is *not* to be treated as an enemy—that is, with hostility—upon arriving in a foreign state. Hospitality to strangers is not a gift or benevolent offering. It is a moral guarantee that is granted by virtue of the stranger's intrinsic dignity as a free being, and denied only if the stranger *gives up* their freedom, arriving in utter hostility. As mentioned in the introduction, this is precisely what makes Kant's understanding of hospitality conditional: if the stranger arrives hostilely, then they can be turned away.

As Robin May Schott notes, hospitality so construed involves refusing to treat an alien as a prisoner (i.e., detaining them), but rather to treat them as a person.[2] And in addition to this, as outlined in the previous passage, if the foreigner will be destroyed upon returning to the place from which he came, it is the duty of the host to not turn them away—that is, to not send them back to a situation that would violate their dignity. This point underlines how forward-thinking Kant was. (We have not achieved universal hospitality yet.) That being said, this does not mean that the foreigner automatically becomes a member of the new "household," but is in fact a guest, just visiting. The other remains distinct. The implications for immigration as we understand it today—especially in regard to displaced peoples, or people fleeing domestic violence—are clear. We have a duty to host the dispossessed; they have a right (as human beings) to be hosted. We will return to this important discussion later.

The final portion of the preceding passage is particularly rich. Kant grounds the right of hospitality in the incontestable fact that in relation to the earth, we are all equal members: "originally no one had more right than another to be on a place on earth." From a certain perspective, we are all members of the same community, called to coexist and therefore host each other. In light of our current ecological crisis, the implications here are also quite obvious. We find ourselves in one home with common resources and we are called to share, whether we like it or not. This involves hospitableness not only to those who are other than oneself but also to those who lie beyond domestic borders. The earth belongs to all of us, equally.

For Kant, therefore, each person, and each nation *qua* collective of persons, has a right to appear before others in hospitality by virtue of their dignity, their freedom, their being counted as a person. Kant goes on to describe the horror of the inhospitable behavior of "civilized" Europeans to those on other continents—behavior justified by an understanding that those inhabitants were *no one*. Preempting Martin Luther King Jr.'s famous quote that "injustice anywhere is a threat to justice everywhere," Kant writes, "the violation of right on one place of earth is felt in all," as humanity itself is undermined (8:360). Violence to any instantiation of humanity amounts to violence toward humanity as a whole, which is to say that hostility to one is in fact hostility to all.

It is important to underline that a key motivating factor in Kant's ethics of hospitality is providing a moral principle that is defined by the absolute exclusion of the calculation of ends. Or in other words, Kant seeks to undermine moral schemas governed by the Machiavellian precept that, as far as action goes, the ends justify the means. As he puts it in the *Critique of Practical Reason*, the "empiricism of practical reason" is the most serious threat to morality because it destroys the root of moral dispositions by placing good and evil in experiential consequences (for example, projections of happiness as the sum total of all our inclinations). This mode of proceeding aims to guarantee projected ends, thus attempting to eliminate the possibility of the unanticipated. Quoting Kearney, it attempts to eliminate "Wonder, surprise, the shock of the new"; it attempts to silence, in Derrida and

Benjamin's terms, the untranslatable kernel ("the messianic")—resistant to what does not fall into one's preexisting schemas.

Despite the fact that *Perpetual Peace* was written ten years after the *Groundwork*, I would contend that is important to consider key aspects of it while analyzing Kant's ethical texts, as Kant's vision of a cosmopolitan constitution,[3] grounded in his understanding of what is best understood as universal human rights, in fact frames and makes sense of his pre-political texts. Kant's aim is to facilitate humanity's movement toward an international state of perpetual peace. That is, one in which morality (theory) is actualized and married with politics (practice). Essential for our purposes is that the principle of hospitality—*the right to not be turned away, the right to not be met with hostility, the right to visit*—plays a vital role in the possibility of peace. It is one of three *sufficient* conditions for perpetual peace.

Noteworthy in Kant's approach in *Perpetual Peace* is that the condition of peace is not natural (for Kant, much like Hobbes, the state of nature is a state of war), but must be constructed, cultivated, and practiced. The mere suspension of hostilities among nations—*agreeing to disagree*, for example, while establishing a peace pact—simply preserves the constant threat of future hostility, even if the outbreak of that hostility never occurs (8:349). For Kant, the threat of future hostility (e.g., housing a standing military during a time of peace) itself undermines any hope for lasting peace, sending a message that the state is in fact *hostile*, ready to defend itself at a moment's notice. This is to say that the refusal to hear the other's convictions (convinced that they are *wrong*, not to be trusted, misguided, evil, and so on) maintains a general disposition of *hostility*: one is perpetually on guard, preparing for future conflict, steadfast in their current ideology, which entails an understanding of us versus them—that is, we are, and must continue to be, superior to them. To be hostile is to be on the defense, perpetually be ready for war. As Hobbes rightly points out in the *Leviathan*, war is not only battle but also living without security.

In the appendix to *Perpetual Peace*, Kant briefly examines the relationship between morality and politics (theory and practice), claiming that it would be absurd to have established the moral law (as he already had) and then claim that acting from duty—and thus in hospitality to the other—is impossible. As Kant writes, "Politics says, '*Be ye wise as serpents*'; morality adds (as a limiting condition) '*and guileless as doves*'" (8:370). Kant not only thinks it is possible to actualize the moral law—which, as we will see, entails actualizing a disposition of hospitality rather than hostility—but he also thinks that true politics cannot proceed without paying homage to the moral law and the honesty it necessitates. The trouble, of course, is that the political moralist pays homage to the maxim: *augment your power in whatever way you see fit.* For Kant, the moral law—here, the concept of right—always comes first, no matter the consequences. Thus, when enacting hospitality, act only in accord with maxims that could become universal laws; treat others never as a mere means, but always as ends in themselves; and respect the dignity (autonomy, freedom, moral law) in others and oneself that secures our status (all of humanity) as *ends*, regardless of the color of their skin, their country of origin—regardless of any empirical, contingent, conditional data whatsoever.

Kant's meditations on what would be required for perpetual peace illuminates his dedication to constructing a moral metalanguage (universal to any and every human being, regardless of their empirical context), and reveals that hospitality is a condition for the possibility of a virtuous society—that is, one in which all of its members are on the way to flourishing. It also reveals that hospitality is the condition for the possibility of truly exercising the moral law, thus honoring the freedom of others (*beyond all forms of empirical borders*), and ceding the fact that we share a world with others, who, like ourselves, want to be free. This point is crucial; hospitality is an expression of respect.

Sharing the World with Others

This notion of sharing the world with others—and more precisely, with a disposition of hospitality, rather than hostility—is, I think, a fruitful way of understanding what Kant calls the "fact of reason" in the *Critique of Practical Reason* (5:31).

Because Kant decides that a deduction of the moral law will not work in the way he hoped it would in the *Groundwork*, he changes his strategy and instead illustrates what it is to (nonempirically) cognize the moral law.[4] Or, borrowing Ricoeur's terms, what it is to cognize *oneself as another*. As Kant portrays it, practical reason inevitably hits a crossroads in which it can either do something in pursuit of satisfying a particular inclination (enslaved to a given hypothetical imperative), or it can act from duty, and thus do something for its own sake (obeying the categorical imperative). The "fact of reason" is Kant's way of denoting what it is to experience the tension between acting from duty (for the other, in hospitality) and acting from inclination (for oneself, in hostility).

Another way of thinking about what Kant means by the fact of reason is that the call of duty—for our purposes, the call to hospitality—is an incontestable fact. It is recognizing that acting from duty involves understanding oneself as a part of a community. That is, recognizing that existence is not just mine, but *ours*. My self-interested pursuits are disrupted, so to speak, by the possibility of acting from duty *qua* understanding myself as a part of the moral community: a moral community that is to be respected and preserved for its own sake. To experience the call to hospitality is to be disrupted from one's self-interested pursuit.

In the second *Critique*, Kant provides an illuminating phenomenological account of finding oneself at the crossroads, *as host*, between hostility and hospitality when "encountering" humanity in the other. That is, experiencing the fact of reason *qua* the possibility of acting from duty (rather than self-interest)—motivated by what he calls the "incentive" of pure practical reason. I would contend that this account should be understood as a phenomenological description of the *desire* to act *in hospitality* from duty, albeit a form of desire that is distinct from an inclination to move toward a given end. That is, a desire pertaining, at least for Kant, to our *rational* rather than *human* nature.

Kant begins his account by asking in what sense (if any) the moral law becomes a subjective determining ground for the will, especially if it cannot be empirical, since we do not actually encounter humanity in experience. Kant stresses that the only way to understand a nonempirical incentive like this is by investigating its effects, rather than that which it supplies itself, as this would be impossible because it (the moral law) is, empirically speaking, nowhere to be found (5:72). Humanity is not an object of cognition since it lacks a corresponding intuition (sense data).

While one might understand Kant's depiction of respect as fear-induced humiliation (as he at moments describes it in precisely this way),[5] it is important to keep in mind that this is only one aspect of the phenomenon. The humiliating dimension is specific to self-conceit. What is humbled is the ego *qua* me-on-my-pursuit-of-happiness. And in that humility, the ego is provoked to, as Kant puts it, *pay tribute*, to offer gratitude, to act in hospitality, which ultimately denotes relinquishing the pride that comes with projecting consequences and believing that those projections are determinate. There is, without question, fear—and therefore hostility—involved in encountering that which has no determined empirical correlate, that is, *the unknown*, and when at the crossroads of decision, one truly does not know what will happen once one acts, as there is no end in sight other than acting from duty. Hostility is perhaps best understood as fear of the other that has turned into a defense or resistance from encountering otherness, be it another person, another culture, another course of action (perhaps that one has never tried before), or simply the unknowable future.

Important for Kant is that when we react to our fear of the unknown with hostility (rather than hospitality), resisting it, we run the risk of constructing seemingly determined consequences that, in reality, may or may not happen. This effectively misses the *exalting* aspect of respect: the power that comes with recognizing that we cannot know with certainty the consequences of our actions. The contingency involved in hypothetical imperatives necessarily rests on probability. And while probability can be a pragmatic guide, Kant's reminder is that, in the end, we really do not know how things will unfold—and being honest about, and hospitable to, this fact is actually empowering, as it provides a window of insight into what we can and cannot know, what is and is not in our power.

Crucial to Kant's account is that the effect of encountering the moral law simultaneously involves pain and exaltation. Affectively, one is humbled in recognizing the prospect of ignoring one's duty to the other, that is, hostilely turning one's back on the other, shutting the door to the needs of the other. The positive aspect of respect involves self-esteem—recognizing that the instantiation of the power of the moral law in *another* is a mirror of the power of the moral law in oneself. One "witnesses" humanity in the sense of understanding oneself as the others—and thus wanting to protect autonomy in both the other and oneself—and ultimately in all of the moral community's constituents.

While Kant describes this affect in a way that leads one to understand it as looking up at the law on high, it is perhaps better to understand this affective phenomenon as experiencing an *immediate shift* from one mode of understanding oneself to another—that is, a shift from hostility to hospitality; a shift from understanding oneself as an individual in the relentless pursuit of happiness to an individual understanding oneself as one among others in the moral collective, ready and willing to let go of one's agenda of happiness so as to preserve the free activity of the whole. Crucial for Kant is that the movement to act hospitably from duty, ultimately provoked by respect, is not the diminishment of activity, but a transfer of activity. Certain hindrances to self-esteem (barriers to understanding oneself as a member of humanity) are removed, and one can act in and through a new understanding of oneself as one-with-the-others.

The incentive of practical reason is, as Kant puts it, a "springing" that has no material object. Rather than a desire to pursue an end—that is, something, spatially or temporally outside of oneself—it is a desire to "let be," "be-with," and, most important, "be free." For Kant, there is a moral-rational desire that mirrors inclination, but is distinct in the sense that it has no object (for inclinations always have desired objects), which means that it does not spring from attempting to satisfy a lack. It does not seek any *thing* in particular, but is instead an elevation, fulfillment, inspiration, and movement provoked by something it cannot grasp or perceive. Again, I think this (no *thing* in particular) can be understood as encountering, being face-to-face with, the untranslatable kernel that Derrida and Benjamin have in mind—the "something more" that inevitably falls outside of what we know with certainty, "transcendence." This experience commands reason to respect the freedom, dignity, and something more of the guest at the border, as well as oneself as host.

Freedom and Desire

Beyond this, it seems clear that the desire for the moral law is Kant's way of describing our desire to be free, which is secured by respecting the moral law. Although, by Kant's account, we cannot prove how freedom is possible, we also cannot help but understand ourselves as practically free. We are called to choose. And in the end, freedom (revealed to us in the experience of respect) is what we desire: "*it has an influence on the human heart so much more powerful than all other incentives, which may be derived from the empirical field. Reason in the consciousness of its dignity despises such incentives and is able gradually to become their master*" (4:411). In the end, we do not want to be slaves to inclination or the will of others; and, returning to Kant's remarks in *Perpetual Peace*, to enslave another is to enslave humanity—including oneself, despite oneself. This is to say that in the end, we actually desire to act in hospitality, to open the door, to let the other appear, to let the other have a voice—in the same way one would want it for oneself.

By Kant's account, in order for freedom to be freedom—that is, for freedom to be free from natural, causal necessity, and preserved as absolute spontaneity—it cannot be bound by time. This means that in every moment of decision, the self *leaps* into something undetermined, unpredictable, *new*. It is actually helpful to think of Kierkegaard's conception of the self here if we are to better understand what exactly it means to *host the strange* in this way. For Kierkegaard, we are a synthesis of what is infinite/indeterminate and what is finite/determined, and we are defined by the way in which we relate to the relation between those two "poles."[6] Being juxtaposed between finitude (causal necessity, the sensible world) and infinitude (possibility, the intelligible world) is what fuels the experience of *being able*. At the moment of decision, one is not necessarily bound to anything that happened before, and, if one is honest with oneself, one has no idea of what will come after. At the moment of decision, one can choose to be otherwise than self-interested, or one can of course choose to bind oneself to the past and the future by projecting what will *likely* come after (based on the past). At the moment of decision, therefore, one can *either* keep one's feet firmly planted on the ground, standing with conviction beside their projection of what will likely happen if one were to do X instead of Y, *or* one can surrender to the fact that one does not know what will happen: humbly accepting that the only thing we truly have control over is our intention.

This is to say that the self, as host, endowed with the power and freedom to welcome or refuse the strange or stranger, affectively *leaps into the unanticipated*—letting go of what can and cannot be controlled. And this leap involves, at least in some sense, a suspension of time, as one suspends anticipated ends. Or, put differently, it involves a lack of consciousness of the future's successive relation to the past—undetermined by what occurred before. Acting-in-hospitality is in this sense timeless, as it acts without regard to the protection of one's future or one's hoped-for interests. Crucial for Kant, as is the case for Kierkegaard (despite his critique of the Kantian-Hegelian ethical mode of being), is that freedom does not know the consequences. And who we are when we host others are freedoms that *know not what we do* in the sense that we do not and cannot know the chain of effects that will flow from this relation to the other, no matter how likely certain outcomes are.[7] Life constantly humbles us with shocking, surprising, unpredictable outcomes, comprising things that we could not have imagined because they have not happened before. They are new. Every guest is a stranger as well as a visitor. And here we arrive at Kant's notion of morality as that which involves the cessation of calculation; the ground for morality involves hospitality to what is new—a twofold hospitality: to the disruption of calculated consequences for oneself, and to the liberty and alterity of others.

While of course distinct from what Derrida has in mind with unconditional hospitality, discussed in Part I, there is something unconditionally hospitable about the moral law itself: there are no exceptions to the rule, no individual cases, no particular circumstances in which this orientation does not apply, no projected consequences that make hospitality to the dignity of the other *immoral*, unless the other has effectively given up their dignity by becoming a criminal, in which case their dignity needs to be properly restored (via some form of corrective education).[8] That being said, the restoration of dignity nonetheless requires welcoming the latent dignity in the other, believing that regardless of the barrier they may face, they can always choose to be autonomous, to choose a disposition of hospitality. Choice is a defining feature of Kantian hospitality.

With that in mind, vital to Kant's account is, as noted, that the past and the future do not define us—at least not completely. Although memory lends itself to certain expectations, we can always, at any moment, choose to act otherwise. For Kant, acquiring *personhood* is choosing freedom in the sense of freeing ourselves from the machinery of nature by elevating ourselves from the sensible world. To be unmoved movers is to be able to bring new things into the world, and to not be governed by hostility toward what is unexpected.

Considering Kant's context, it is not surprising that he wants to preserve a space for innovation, creativity, and progress—all of which, for him, are necessarily secured by freedom's possibility. In "What Is Enlightenment?" Kant famously cries for mankind to awaken from its self-incurred immaturity: to dare to know, and to have the courage to use our understanding (8:35). Kant wants humanity to release itself from the shackles of religious dogma (religious devotees as paradigmatic instances of what he means by heteronomy of the will), to not be afraid of shadows, and to think freely, so as to host new phenomena, new discoveries, new modes of being—like that of a truly just society or international perpetual peace, made possible by acting in hospitality toward what is alien, different, strange.

It is ultimately in his rendering of freedom in the second *Critique* that we find another response to the "superficiality" of empiricism (5:94), which for Kant inevitably gets no further than a notion of freedom in which one's freedom is that of a "turnspit, which, when once it is wound up, also accomplishes its movements of itself" (5:97). Kant is determined not to reduce human beings to the predictability we find in physics, but he wants to safeguard our capacity to act otherwise than predictions based on behavioral analysis (which, by his account, all point to a sort of pseudo-hedonistic self-interest). This reduction, as Kearney noted previously, is what blinds us to the something more that "enables humans to do the impossible, to break with conditioned patterns of thinking and behavior."

To support this position, Kant describes the phenomenon of holding those who were not fortunate in their childhood education and grow up to be "villains" accountable for their "wickedness" (5:100). This, he claims, is something that we do, and is a testimony of the fact that they are responsible for their decisions, regardless of their context. While this view might seem callous, the flip side of the phenomenon is that these children can change. They can be otherwise. Although, for Kant, they cannot eliminate the guilt they have for wicked past deeds, they can reconstruct their character. By virtue of freedom's possibility, nobody is bound to any behavioral fate or psychology, regardless of how solidified their habits may seem. We can and should expect to be surprised both by others and ourselves, and we should not categorize anyone into a box from which they cannot escape, as this would ignore the will's capacity to shift its orientation, to determine itself anew, that is, the capacity to act as opposed to merely reacting to empirical stimuli.

In light of the notion of hospitality that we find in *Perpetual Peace*, each person by virtue of their freedom has a right to appear before others without being met with hostility. To hospitably allow others to appear in their dignity, autonomy and individuality, is to recognize them as bearers of the moral law. To refuse to shape them into what one wants them to be. The same goes for oneself. To be autonomous is to appear as you are, rather than the way others want you to be. For Kant, the moral self is, therefore, a host who lets others appear as they are—safeguarding, in hospitality, each freedom's voice. And vital for Kant is each dignity *having a voice*, contributing to the conversation, as conversation is the road to growth and peace. As he puts it in his *Lectures on Ethics*:

> Social intercourse is in itself a cultivator of virtue and a preparation for its surer practice. . . . The exchange of our sentiments is the principle factor of social intercourse, and truth must be the guiding principle herein. Without truth social intercourse and conversation become valueless. We can only know what a man thinks if he tells us his thought, and when he understands to express them he must really do so, or else there can be no society of men. Fellowship is only the second condition of society, and a liar destroys fellowship. Lying makes it impossible to derive any benefit in conversation. (198–224)

Kant stresses that the proclivity to be *reserved* spawns from a desire to conceal one's faults and shortcomings (224)—pretending to be otherwise so that others will understand one to have virtues that one does not in fact have, ultimately to gain more, for one's own sake. Kantian hospitality requires honesty and honest conversation, which in turn requires a suspension of calculation (and all the means and ends that are concealed along the way), a disruption of predictable patterns, an open orientation to the unanticipated, unpredictable, and uncomfortable. As we will see in the chapters that follow, these are all defining features of conversation itself. For conversation to truly be conversation, one must be willing to host the strange.

To further understand Kant's depiction of standing at the crossroads of the fact of reason, it is important to consider Kant's point regarding violations of the categorical imperative as inducing what he somewhat enigmatically calls a contradiction of the will or a contradiction of reason. I think the best way to interpret this is as a self-contradiction, or better, an existential contradiction: experiencing the incentive of practical reason to act from duty, *the desire for justice*, the enticement of *hospitality* toward the autonomy of another, in tension with the desire to satisfy self-conceit, the inclination to actualize hypothetical states of affairs, the temptation of hostility toward the other.[9]

This implies, perhaps unsurprisingly, that the condition for the possibility of overcoming war is choosing hospitality over hostility when face-to-face with the other. Crucial for Kant is that when we act in hospitality, we become less bound to hypothetical contingencies and externalities, and, more important, we become less at war with others (and ultimately ourselves). To move toward freedom is to move toward a greater understanding of what is and is not within our power. The authentic *moral* self is a self who is not only capable of thinking about the other before herself but is also a self who is free from the anxiety that comes with constructing a projected reality that may or may not come to be, which is the result of being hostile toward the unanticipated.

Encountering the moral law in the other ultimately brings the Kantian subject face-to-face with their true self—the experience of respect marking an occasion for a gestalt shift or *conversion*. That is, an opportunity to understand oneself anew: to understand *the others as oneself*, to constitute one's will as good. As Kant notes at the end of the second *Critique*, images of good character reveal the dignity each of us has within ourselves, and that revelation is essential. Echoing the hermeneutic dictum in Part I, the shortest route from self to self is through the other. Quoting Kant:

> And now the law of duty, through the positive worth that observance of it lets us feel, finds easier access through the *respect of ourselves* in the consciousness of our freedom. When this is well established, when a human being dreads nothing more than to find, on self-examination, that he is worthless and contemptible in his own eyes, then every good moral disposition can be grafted onto it, because this is the best, and indeed the sole, guard to prevent ignoble and corrupting impulses from breaking into the mind. (5:161)

Thus, by Kant's account, when we honor any and every inclination, obeying the *modus operandi* that I ought to pursue whatever will bring me closer to what I want right now, the happiness I project, what I think will be the most pleasurable life, we, in fact, isolate ourselves from the moral community, fracturing our sense of community, repressing our desire for justice. Self-conceit as the governing force in one's life leads to extreme isolation, as one starts to conceive of oneself as an island—hostile to anything and everything outside of oneself—understanding the others as nothing other than obstacles in one's pursuit of happiness, or tools to be used in service of one's pursuit of happiness. The call to hospitality disappears, since every effort of the self is for itself. There is nobody worth opening the door to.

To bring this back to our duty to host the dispossessed, given the fact that human beings all (by virtue of being human) have a right to hospitality, the political manifestation of every effort of the self being for itself involves rejecting those who are different. *What do we owe those who lie beyond domestic borders? Am I the stranger's keeper?* Although, as Schott points out, Kant is privy to the issue of immigration, he predates the issue concerning the type of immigration that is motivated by war and genocide.[10] What seems clear, based on the preceding analysis, is that for Kant the immigrant has a right to appear, to have a voice, to be honored in their inalienable dignity as a human being. What we owe those who lie beyond domestic borders is the right to hospitality, and this right becomes more pressing when refugees are running away from violent human rights violations abroad. By Kant's account, morality demands that so long as the stranger arrives peaceably, *if we have a door to open, we ought to open it.* With the categorical imperative's "universalizability" criterion in mind: Would we not hope for the same if we were in their shoes?

As Kant envisions it, what we all desire most is freedom, albeit not freedom in the sense of license to do anything and everything we want to do (as any inclination wishes), but freedom in the sense of continuing to coexist and act in a world with others—a world void of war, slavery, exploitation, and imperialism. This sort of freedom is limiting in the sense that it safeguards space for the freedom of others, which can involve not always getting what one wants. But this sort of freedom is also liberating in its honesty in regard to the significance of the moral community—the membership of which we both need—freeing us from the delusion that the preservation of oneself in one's individual pursuit of happiness (inevitably hostile toward others to some extent) takes precedence over anything and anyone else.

For Kant, acting from duty, thus acting in hospitality, is without question the vehicle by which we can adequately protect the free community—at a global level—that we all intrinsically desire. Our housing of the moral law is another way of understanding the desire we have for justice and peace: *the rational desire to act in hospitality.* Again, whether or not one agrees with the strictures of Kant's moral project, I think it is clear that Kant accurately unveils freedom as an honest orientation toward unpredictability and preserves morality as the suspension of calculation. This is an orientation that is hospitable toward that which is beyond oneself and one's control: above all, the otherness of other people.

6

Impossible Hospitality
From Levinas to Arendt

With the previously sketched hermeneutic of Kantian hospitality in mind (by my interpretation, synonymous with acting from duty), this chapter will analyze the post-Kantian shift to philosophies of hospitality—in particular, Emmanuel Levinas's philosophy of hospitality *par excellence*, but also briefly that of Hannah Arendt, who serves as a middle way between Kant and Levinas. Here we rejoin and amplify the discussion of possible/impossible hospitality in Part I.

As stressed in Part I, Levinas is one of the most important thinkers to explicitly relate ethics to hospitality, going so far as describing the self as, first and foremost, *a host*. As Levinas notoriously writes, "The self is through and through a hostage, older than the ego, prior to principles. What is at stake for the self, in its being, is not to be. Beyond egoism and altruism it is the religiosity of the self . . . Subjectivity is being hostage" (*Otherwise Than Being or Beyond Essence* [hereafter OB] 117, 127). Prior to any willed or free decision in the Kantian sense, Levinas's ethics of hospitality radically insists that the self is always already called "to give to the Other taking the bread out of my mouth, and making a gift of my own skin" (OB, 138). Levinas will invert the modern understanding of the subject, paradoxically exposing what is more primordial than freedom, activity, and passivity in the traditional sense.

This chapter will probe Levinas's original account of *who we are* (exposed, vulnerable, for-others, hosts, hostages, substituting-for-the-other, infinitely responsible) in relation to what makes hospitality as first philosophy *impossible*—namely, that it is not (*contra* Kant) an act of the will or a decision we can make. I will end the chapter by turning to Arendt's more explicitly political (practical or possible) account of what I refer to as "natal hospitality"—a continuation of, and response to, hospitality's perceived impossibility, recasting her notion of natality as a novel way of understanding what it means to host the other and *why*.

Originary Hospitality

With a critical eye toward the atrocities of the twentieth century, Levinas's seminal text *Totality and Infinity* (hereafter TI) notoriously begins with the claim that "one would readily agree that it is of the upmost importance to determine whether we have been duped by morality" (21). He then links the suspension of morality to the ever-present possibility of war:

> Does not lucidity, the mind's openness upon the true, consist in catching sight of the permanent possibility of war? The state of war suspends morality.... In advance its shadow falls over the actions of man. War is not only one of the ordeals—the greatest—of which morality lives; it renders morality derisory. The art of foreseeing war and of winning it by every means—politics—is henceforth enjoined as the very exercise of reason. Politics is opposed to morality, as philosophy to naïveté. (TI, 21)

For Levinas, morality disrupts political ambition (the desire to win, and gain more) in the same sense that philosophy (the desire for wisdom) disrupts naïveté. That is, just as Socrates, in his pursuit of wisdom (and work as a *gadfly*), interrupts the naïveté of his interlocutors, morality, too, interrupts one's political pursuits by throwing into question an "objective order from which there is no escape" (TI, 21): for example, the pain in the face of a child being separated from their "undocumented" mother, prompting one to refuse to participate in the executive order to separate them. In this example, morality's call to hospitality holds one "hostage" to the suffering of the stranger, leaving one utterly incapable of looking away, following the orders one was given, or attending to any aspect of one's own self-interest. It goes without saying that a moment of disruption—heeding hospitality's call, in this case ceasing the perceived violence—is not enough to constitute what Levinas has in mind when he speaks of radical hospitality. For Levinas, the stakes are much higher and are, as noted earlier, in some sense impossible to actually fulfill. The work of an ethics of hospitality is never done, though hospitality's claim is always and already the case.

Despite clear difference with Kant, Levinas's ethics of hospitality can at least partially be understood through Kant's formula of humanity,[1] which involves safeguarding the others as ends that should not be exploited, manipulated, or totalized.[2] I also think it is helpful to understand Levinas's question of whether we have been duped or deceived by morality as an echo of Kant's questioning of whether the supreme, absolute, universally necessary moral principle that he seeks (the condition for the possibility of peace) may, in the end, be nothing more than a chimera: a theoretical dream among philosophers, like that of perpetual peace. Levinas's rhetorical worry is that if we *have* in fact been duped by morality, and morality is in fact nothing more than a dream or myth among philosophers, then hostility or war is our inevitable and total reality. And if war is in fact our total reality, then morality is rendered "derisory," because war, by its very definition, intends the usurpation of the other. And this necessarily entails the transformation of what is different (e.g., an ideology, like "communism," or a category of people, like "communists") into a rendition of the warring force (e.g., an ideology like "democracy," or a category of people, like "democrats").

The most important point for Levinas is that if reality is in fact war, and morality is nothing more than a fiction, then what we are tragically duped into is an alienated understanding of ourselves as "soldiers," who are perpetually in hostility with the others and ourselves. As Levinas puts it, war "destroys the genuine identity of the same" by driving the same to reduce anything and everything other into an extension of itself (TI, 21); war drives its conscripts into an isolated and production-oriented mode of being, which is part and parcel of a disordered understanding of the self that is arguably alive and well in the Anglo-American West, and (as we will see) that Aristotelian virtue ethics is both contesting and attempting to overturn.

Levinas is ultimately interested in evoking an understanding of morality that is not merely something that philosophers hope for, or a principle that we can argue ourselves into endorsing, but is instead something extant—*ontologically* preserved in "metaphysical desire" for the other, which, for Levinas, is the most essential dimension of who we are—"beneath" oneself understood as a self-aware ego, which again, by Levinas's account, denotes the reigning self-reflexive conception of our being.[3] Levinas will integrate hospitality into his rendering of the subject, closing any possible gap that might exist between ethics and metaphysics. The crucial point here is that while an ethics of hospitality is a choice (we can, of course, choose to ignore the call of the other), the claim of hospitality is not. We are always and already called, whether we like it or not.

Perhaps most vital to Levinas's account is that the commands of reason will not deliver our duty to the other. The "ground" of morality is not hiding somewhere within reason (as, for instance, Kant would have it). For Levinas, the source of ethics is sensible, lived, despite not appearing to perception and resisting conceptual thematization. *Sense* always refers to the other, which is "revealed" (albeit always concealed from consciousness) in the face-to-face encounter and the unremitting proximity of the other to me. It is important to point out that in addition to referring to the other person, "the other" denotes any disruption that pulls us out of our reflective, self-conscious selves[4]—our projects, productions, reflections, and expectations. Therefore, in addition to signifying the other person, "the other" can also be understood as the new, the unknown, the unpredictable, or the future, since all of these entail indeterminate content *otherwise than the simple presence of the self to itself* (TI, 35).

By Levinas's account, what is missing from the Western philosophical tradition, epitomized by Kant, is first a concrete understanding of morality that looks "out" (to what is beyond oneself), rather than looking "in" (to the structures of cognition), and second a notion of moral responsibility that has nothing to do with the will (e.g., responsibility as an altruistic act of the will, or form of accountability, or *choice*). Levinas is interested in establishing an ethics of hospitality as first philosophy (metaphysics), which is to say that for Levinas, existence ought to be understood ethically; and responsibility, as an iteration of hospitality—rather than being a willed decision or a debt to pay—is woven into the very fabric of who we are. His morality of hospitality is, therefore, meant to show us that we do not choose to act in hospitality; our very being is constituted by hospitality. We are hosts—and actually desire to be. Levinas therefore is not offering a prescriptive account of ethics or a robust defense of a moral theory, but is instead providing an evocative, phenomenological account of who we are underneath our perceived sense of self-identity; he seeks to unveil our primordial desire for the other: the desire that constitutes one's existence. It is a desire (in his words, *metaphysical desire*) that nourishes itself with its hunger (TI, 34), driven by a pull toward that which one cannot foresee, and without any promise of resolution, only the promise of encountering something new. It is a desire to host the unknown.

Vital to Levinas's account is that the "opening" between the desirer and the desired is never closed. Metaphysical desire, as Levinas construes it, is preserved by the conjunction—the "and"—that inhibits the desirer and desired from constituting a closed system (a totality in which the two are ultimately one). It is this opening that preserves the hunger that gives desire its motor. In light of the debate between Habermas and Derrida discussed at length in Part I, it is helpful to think about the fissure between the desirer and desired through the example of a rich, ongoing conversation between two friends, in which the two friends' perspectives are never fully fused in to one—at least not to the point of one utterly ceasing to be different, since this would then cease to be a relation between one and the other and would instead denote a relation between oneself and oneself. Difference would reduce to sameness. This point about conversation will be elucidated in the following chapter in light of contemporary virtue ethics.

Echoing the themes explored in Part I, despite inching ever closer to the stranger, locating crucial moments or points of similarity, one never fully possesses, grasps, or attains the other's perspectives or interpretations in their entirety. The labor involved in understanding another never ends because the other is never fully exposed: there is always something more, something surprising, something new, something other than what is currently *known*. The untranslatable kernel inevitably remains. Metaphysical desire denotes that pull toward the other and can be understood as *originary hospitality*. That is, our primordial openness to what is other than ourselves, our primordial movement toward that which we cannot imagine or foresee, the innate drive that fuels narrative exchange and healing.

The "Subject" as Sensibility

For Levinas, sensibility—most essentially constituted by flesh and touch, in Bettina Bergo's words, "'epidermal' vulnerability"[5]—denotes who we most fundamentally are. We are, first and foremost, embodied and sensing: "subjects" subjected—hosts, hostages—to what is outside of ourselves, constantly fissured and interrupted. This is a conception of the self that is ultimately affected and constituted by the world, rather than affecting and constituting the world (as, for instance, Kant would have it).[6] This is a conception of the self as originary hospitality, or in Kearney's terms, *carnal hospitality*. Sensibility signifies the openness, undergoing, susceptibility of one's flesh—pure exposure without dwelling or "somewhere" to hide: *skin laid bare*. Sensibility signifies subjectivity as hospitality, holding the door open—utterly exposed—to what is other than oneself. For Levinas, it is in this sense that sensibility signifies my irreplaceability as one-for-the-other, or put differently, my responsibility for the other. My response-ability—that is, my responsiveness, by default, to the experiences that I undergo—cannot be given to somebody else. It is in this sense that sensibility as responsibility constitutes *me*. It is not unreasonable to suggest that in Levinas's schema, in some sense similar to what we find in Kant (save the role of reason) responsibility and hospitality are interchangeable terms.

Sensibility is the experience of being in one's skin, enfleshed, touching or being in contact with things. As we saw in Kearney's depiction of carnal hospitality, to be is to be tactile and sensate.[7] To be *alive* is to touch what is outside of us, to be in relation-to . . . X; and to touch is to be utterly exposed, at perpetual risk. For Levinas, sensibility marks the forgetting of self-concern, albeit not by an act of the will, but as being seized—held hostage, persecuted—by the other. This seizure from self-concern, by Levinas's account, constitutes freedom in the most authentic sense: that is, freedom as hospitality, rather than freedom as a self-determining act of the will:

> Freedom is animation itself, breath, the breathing outside air, where inwardness frees itself from itself, and is exposed to all winds. There is exposure without assumption, which would already be closedness. That the emptiness of space would be filled with invisible air, hidden from perception, save in the caress of the wind or the threat of storms, non-perceived, but penetrating me even in my retreats of inwardness, that this invisibility or this emptiness would be breathable or horrible, that this invisibility is non-indifferent and obsesses me before all thematization, that the simple ambiance is imposed as an atmosphere to which the subject gives himself and exposes himself in his lungs, without intentions and aims, that the subject could be a lung at the bottom of substance—all this signifies a subjectivity that suffers and offers itself before taking a foothold in being. It is a passivity, wholly a supporting. (OB, 180)

To be clear, the affective undergoing of sensible hospitality is prior to the "I think," or reflective self-consciousness's representation of objective content to itself. The self as sensibility is a self exposed to, open before, and in contact with what is outside of reflective consciousness. The sensible self is a self without will, without intention, without a projected end or aim in mind. The self of sensibility is moved by, and thus responsible for, as responsive to, what is outside of itself. And again, this is a notion of responsibility that has nothing to do with resolve or accountability, but rather the impossibility of evading assignment by the other—of evading hospitality. As Judith Butler aptly puts it, ethical responsibility presupposes *responsiveness*.[8] And her salient Levinasian point is that we are not only responsible for what we consent to.

Essential for Levinas is that sensibility, in perpetual proximity to what is other than oneself, has the ontological structure of being-one-for-another. "Proximity" is Levinas's way of describing the contact that is not already parsed into a duality of receptive sensor (known subject) and a received sensed (determined object). Proximity denotes our immediate exposure to and experience of things other than ourselves, as well as the non-indifference one has toward what is *next to, up against, in contact with* oneself, which can of course be enjoyable or painful (OB, 90). The important point is that we only experience ourselves in reflection (concerning ourselves with ourselves). When immersed in experience, what we experience is activity: the reflective self ultimately disperses into the activity itself (e.g., feeling cool in the sea). We can of course reflect on the experience, but once reflection starts, one realizes one was "lost" in the experience.

Sensibility so construed plays a vital role in Levinas's schema, because ontologically speaking, its structure is that of living-from-the-other, albeit existing-for-the-other: absolutely exposed, and thus hospitable to what is beyond oneself. *To be sensate is to host.* Sensibility denotes the affective undergoing that is intrinsic to existence. To be "nude" in one's skin is to exist for, to be moved by, what is other than oneself. What is inseparable from who one *is* is one's corporeality (OB, 78),[9] which is ultimately animated, inspired, incarnated, hosted *from without*, for example, being birthed into existence by another, inhaling and exhaling air, being nourished by food, and so on.

Self-consciousness, for Levinas, is the result of experiencing the insecurity intrinsic to sensibility.[10] That is, the risk of being wounded, of experiencing pain, that inescapably accompanies exposure. This is a risk that sensibility does not notice until it is wounded in a way that drives it to retreat, so as to attempt to avoid (in hostility) future suffering. To avoid future suffering requires calculation: identifying means that will secure the identified end (i.e., avoid pain). Consciousness is therefore born once one's vulnerability is recognized and reflected upon. Its anxiety about the possibility of future pain drives it to withdraw from the world upon which it depends, and thus build a dwelling closed to strangers, to try and escape the anxiety *of the morrow*: the unpredictability of the future, what is not determined. Once it retreats into its newfound dwelling, the host begins to recollect itself (marking the birth of concern), shifting into the world of intentionality, conscious perception.

The important takeaway here is that by Levinas's account, inner experience (self-consciousness, the "I") is necessarily conditioned by outer experience (the world beyond oneself). Hospitality comes before the decision to open the door or not. Self-consciousness—including volition—does not come first. For Levinas, following an underappreciated point in Kant's theoretical work,[11] outer sense is ontologically prior.[12] Thus, the self as sensibility (outer sense) marks who we are in the most fundamental sense, whereas the self as self-conscious reflection (inner sense)—the self of predications, judgments, propositions, and calculations—is the result of anxiously being thrust back onto oneself because of the fear of the other *qua* unknown, uncertain. The subject as subjected (sensibility, host) precedes the subject as agent (self-consciousness, hostile to potential pain).

This crucial point distinguishes Levinas from both Derrida and Kant, whose schemas rely on an account of hospitality that presupposes autonomy: that is, a willed choice to open the door or not. Levinas is uniquely reclaiming the aspect of hospitality that has nothing to do with the will—a passivity beyond passivity "beneath" the familiar act/potency pair. Once we become self-conscious subjects, autonomously navigating through the world—hosts in Derrida's sense of the term: masters of a house with a door that can open or close, if we so choose—we can of course choose to ignore what we hear, blind ourselves to suffering, become deaf to the call for help. But for Levinas—and this is where he is distinct, and the radical-impossible nature of his work really shows—moral sense remains and is always already the case. For Levinas, even if a *response* to the other is not automatic, the claim of the other is. Levinas is, above all, committed to retrieving this primordial aspect of experience.

With the previous chapter in mind, a crucial point for our purposes is that both Kant and Levinas are committed to a sense of morality that involves *hospitably* holding open a space for and thus cherishing transcendence—and again, transcendence in the sense of what is not immanently present to conscious reflection. That is, the *something more* that perpetually falls through our finger tips. This is what ultimately constitutes the dignity of the other, the source of their own unique voice. Although Levinas does not understand who we are in the same way that Kant does (for whom we are, above all, rational agents), he similarly emphasizes that we are more than the productive, predictable, self-aware modes of being that have been overemphasized by the temper of our production-oriented times. For both Kant and Levinas, morality involves the cessation of means-ends calculation before what is other. That is, hospitality to the strange.

Within this vein, the most crucial difference between the two thinkers is of course that for Levinas, morality is not a conscious, reflective act of the will. And this is precisely what makes Levinasian hospitality (in Derrida's "unconditional" sense) impossible.[13] For Levinas, an ethics of hospitality cannot involve an active choice on the part of the subject—for example, *choosing* altruism—which is why he insists on a metaphysical understanding of moral responsibility. This is to say that the crucial distinction for Levinas is not between acting from duty/in hospitality and acting from inclination/in hostility, but instead between willing the good and *being subjected to the good*. For Levinas, we are always and already responsible, always and already hosting; the other has made its claim on each and every one of us, whether we are comfortable with it or not. The subject as host, hospitality, is the *original goodness of creation*.

One of the most important points, therefore, to take from Levinas's ethics of hospitality is that I am not the origin of ethics, I am not the origin of myself. Any obsession with one's own self-worth, one's own existence before death, and one's own destiny is derisory, tragic, even comic, as it is a "willed" forgetting of the good. This will never cease to disrupt us in our self-interested pursuits insofar as we exist. The good is precisely the forgetting of oneself in being-for-the-other, substituting for the other, being otherwise than in sync with an agenda; in Levinas's words, the extraordinary forgetting of death that is not ignorance of death. The good, which is the source of all meaning whatsoever, flows from the breakdown of unity and consistency. I will never find it within myself, and it is not something I am on the way to. The good is immanent-as-transcendent in the encounter with the other. And while encountering the good can be traumatic, the "pain" is not painful in itself—we simply judge it to be so. Learning may involve suffering, but it is a suffering soon forgotten in the ecstasy of relinquishing self-concern and truly being-for-the-other.

Thus, despite ourselves, the other affects us—obsesses us—from the start (OB, 129). Despite ourselves, we are called to host the stranger. As Butler stresses in her account of Levinasian ethics, receptivity is not only a precondition for action, but one of its constituent features: "What is unchosen in the force of the image articulates something about ethical obligations that impose themselves upon us without our consent."[14] Again, we can of course choose to be otherwise (concerned predominantly with ourselves, *hostile* to alterity), rejecting an ethics of hospitality, but hospitality's claim is not a choice. The subject is, from minute one, subjected. As Levinas writes:

> Obedience precedes any hearing of the command. The possibility of finding, anachronously, the order in the obedience itself, and of receiving the order out of oneself, this reverting of heteronomy into autonomy, is the very way the Infinite passes itself. The metaphor of inscription of the law in consciousness expresses this in a remarkable way, reconciling autonomy and heteronomy. It does so in an ambivalence, whose diachrony is the signification itself, an ambivalence, which, in the present, is an ambiguity. The inscription of the order in the for-the-other of obedience is an anarchic being affected, which slips into me "like a thief" through the outstretched nets of consciousness.... This ambivalence is the exception and subjectivity of the subject, its very psyche, a possibility of inspiration. It is the possibility of being the author of what had been breathe in unbeknownst to me, of having received, one knows not from where, that of which I am the author. In the responsibility for the other we are at the heart

of the ambiguity of inspiration. The unheard-of saying is enigmatically in the anarchic response, in my responsibility for the other. (OB, 148–149)

Although Kant is pushing up against an understanding of morality as an undergoing—being called, in the experience of respect for the moral law, to *let go* of self-conceit—Kant nonetheless holds fast to a sense of autonomy that involves consciously constituting oneself morally, commanding the will to be good. That being said, what is clearly latent in Kant's account of respect is that despite the fact that respect occurs within me *I am not the origin of that affect*. It is the moral law in *another* that shakes me from without, awakening what lies "within" myself as a potentially hospitable subject. As Levinas suggests himself, what we find in Kant is the reverting of heteronomy to autonomy: I become the origin because the origin is forgotten, as it is not available to memory, or conscious reflection (OB, 148). Levinas's account is "impossible" in the sense that it is absolutely unconditional, which is to say that one does not decide to be hospitable, to be exposed, to open the door. There is no choice in the matter, no "why," no rationale. That being said, as Richard Kearney rightly stresses, practically speaking we cannot help but make a choice—to *wager*—when encountering the face of the other. To act otherwise would be untenable and, in extreme cases, disastrous.

Natal Hospitality

It is here that I will briefly turn to Hannah Arendt as a helpful post-Kantian alley (albeit still sympathetic to Kant)—someone who provides a political/practical/possible way of understanding hospitality through her notion of natality.[15] Arendt offers a middle way between Kant and Levinas in the sense that she is committed to universal human rights, but rather than grounding it in in rationality, she grounds it in something that looks like singularity as depicted in Part I, and sensibility as depicted here. In her terms: *natality*.

Though hospitality is not thematized in Arendt's work in the same way we find it thematized in other thinkers, her concern about the rights of those who do not belong to any political entity, that is, the right of the stateless to have rights (*qua* member of humanity), is a call to welcome the alien, host the refugee, and, as we saw in Kant, secure a space for newcomers to appear without being met with hostility. Arendt is critical of Kant's failure to account for particularity in his meditations on morality, but she deeply admires his insistence on impartiality.[16] For Arendt, the right to have rights ought to be guaranteed by simply being a member of the human species—with the capacity for action: that is, speech and deed. But she is careful to point out that this guarantee is often stifled by the fact that national rights are what guarantee human rights, which is limited by borders and law.[17]

Despite infamously not understanding herself as a philosopher (in the sense of contemplating being or human nature), I think that it is reasonable to suggest that natality is Arendt's answer to the question: *What is being*? For Arendt, *to be* is *to begin*, to be birthed, and, most importantly, to freely birth new things—that is, is to bring (through speech and deed) the new, the surprising, *the strange* into the world. Natality is loosely defined as the uniqueness that "distinguishes every human being from every other, the quality by virtue of which he is not only a stranger in the world but something that has never been here before."[18] Natality is the source of each human being's *right to have rights*—simply by virtue of belonging to humanity, and regardless of whether one belongs to a particular state.[19] In Arendt's world, natality is precisely what we ought to respect and thus be hospitable to. Arendt is therefore providing an account of what we could call *natal hospitality*: acknowledging and respecting (much like Kant) the dignity-*qua*-natality of each person.

For Arendt, the meaning of natality is at least twofold: the physical birth of the child, and then being a political being by birthing speech and deeds. What is involved in giving birth to something new is having no idea what happens next. Birth involves utter unexpectedness and unpredictability: *strangeness*. Part of Arendt's scathing critique of the alienation of the modern age is that in the wake of Cartesian doubt, we have become completely hostile to anything and everything that is otherwise than a foreseeable or predictable product. For her, the modern age is that in which calculating, predicting, knowing what comes next, and being sure of what necessarily follows from a given premise reign supreme. Logic is one of our beloved authorities, sitting comfortably next to pattern-based moral theories. Thus, modernity, as Arendt understands it, is perhaps even defined by an explicit rejection of natal hospitality in its attempt to squash randomness, strangeness, and the unpredictable.

To relate this to Levinas's conception of who we are, my claim is that natality is another way of articulating Levinas's notion of being-as-sensibility: utter exposure or radical openness, being-as-hospitality, being before the other(s). And in regard to Kant, for Arendt, natality is the source of human dignity; it is another way of understanding Kantian autonomy. What she has in mind specifically is being before the other, expressing one's singularity through speech and deed. Thus, for Arendt, when you truly act, you are radically open, and therefore honest. And when you are honest, you realize you have no control beyond that expression, meaning you have no control over the consequences. You genuinely do not know what comes next—and welcome that fact, partaking in natal hospitality.[20] That is, hospitality to the strange. The opposite disposition would therefore involve, out of fear and hostility, retreating into a world of consistency: predictable patterns and behaviors, the pursuit and preservation of certainty by any means.

To return to the question of moral psychology/human motivation, it is worth pointing out that the banality of evil—as Arendt reports in *Eichmann in Jerusalem* and thoroughly fleshes out in "Thinking and Moral Considerations"—markedly involves the inability to hear another voice, including the voice within oneself (conscience). This is an utter rejection of the stranger and any strangeness such voices entails. The only remedy to evil, at least as Arendt understands it, is *thinking*: an activity that is distinct from knowing, and, despite being somewhat atypical, is by no means impossible. It is the very possible reflective quest for meaning that is, for her, epitomized by Socrates, whose life almost solely consisted in thinking (as she understands it)—incessantly dialoging with himself and his friends, perpetually soliciting ever more points of view, and unrelenting in the face of *aporia*. Socrates is always ready to be surprised by hosting the strange.

Ethically speaking, Arendt thinks our unthinking acceptance of utilitarianism, at least in practice, is symptomatic of this tendency toward calculation and certainty: it is the mathematical, empirical moral theory *par excellence*. By Arendt's account, philosophy suffered more from modernity than any other field of study. The discipline, as we know it, is still trapped in the Cartesian nightmare: that is, a fundamental skepticism, grounded in hostility toward the strange. For Arendt, this mistrust constitutes the depravity of human kind. And by mistrust, she means the doubt we have in our adequacy to receive anything true, and our general mistrust of each other—that is, our hostility toward the fact of plurality, plurality here referring to the fact that, as she puts it in *The Human Condition*, "men, not Man, live on the earth and inhabit the world" (7). This sentiment of course fuels the type of racism and, more broadly, xenophobia that make exclusion, exception, and, in extreme cases, extermination possible. The opposite, hospitality, warrants the possibility of participating and creating with "a plurality of others," by allowing thinking to cross borders.[21] As Robin May Schott points out, when we are able to think beyond borders, to empathize with the stranger, "differences can be imaginatively overcome," and we are more likely to then argue and fight for their (legal) rights—at the very least, basic levels of "alien" protection.[22]

Thinking, as Arendt understands it, is the way in which we enter into the realm of what Kearney and Ricoeur call narrative hospitality: that is, a mode of thinking that involves trying to see the world through the lens of the other, despite the fact that this is not something we can definitively do. I will never be able to literally walk or fit in somebody else's shoes, though I can of course, by way of narrative imagination, work to understand *what it is like* to walk in those shoes—albeit never assuming them as my own (a dangerous business for the reasons we saw in Part I). I can, through narrative exchange, host them and their unique perspective, listen and learn. With our definition of an ethics of radical hospitality in mind (embracing complexity, diversity, the unexpected rather than prematurely endorsing accepted norms), the activity of thinking—which is not guided by practical *purposes*, is good *for* nothing (beyond itself), is perpetually uncertain[23]—does not shirk in the face of complexity and is never fully convinced. And it is never fully convinced in the sense that it acknowledges that there is always more than meets the eye. There is always a surplus, a *something more*.

With the insights from Part I in mind, occasioning natality—rebirth—is a fundamental dimension of Arendt's understanding of narrative.[24] According to Arendt, one's own narrative reveals things about oneself that one cannot see, but others can—and provides a chance for two distinct human beings to hospitably share the world. Narrative is a vehicle for meaning to be revealed in a sense that does not define or "give it all away," so to speak, while still providing the opportunity to imagine the world of another and thus shape conscience. For Arendt, narrative captures the *sui generis* of action,[25] and the way it (*qua* natality) shatters predictable patterns and dogmas, thereby helping us open ourselves to the stranger and the strange, and thus share the world. *Narrative fosters natal hospitality.* The important point here is that by Arendt's account, we find meaning in birth, which entails novelty, the unexpected, the unanticipated—that which strikes awe and wonder. Or in the terms of this volume, hosting the strange illuminates moral meaning, which is vital to both living well and avoiding evil.

By Arendt's account (echoing Kant in the first *Critique*), human beings love to think beyond the limits of knowledge.[26] And what lies beyond the limits of knowledge is nothing other than the strange, *the new*. To indulge this desire—that is, to indulge natal hospitality by hosting the strange—is not only possible via narrative exchange and otherwise, but, as we will see in the next chapter, is also part of a full and flourishing human life. Despite the fact that natal hospitality does not know what comes next, does not condition itself by potential consequences, it remains a crucial dimension of practical wisdom.

Teleological Hospitality
The Case of Contemporary Virtue Ethics

With Kant's hospitality beyond borders, Levinas's "impossible" hospitality, and Arendt's natal hospitality as a middle way in mind, this chapter will explore what I take to be the post-Kantian possible ethics *par excellence*: contemporary virtue ethics. In the spirit of Aristotle, contemporary virtue ethics seeks to provide an account of ethics that is relevant to life, as we know it—and for our purposes, an ethics of hospitality that is more than theory. Elaborating on what has been covered thus far, I will critically interpret Talbot Brewer's remarkably comprehensive Aristotelian-inspired approach to reimagining the task of moral philosophy and the moral philosopher, ultimately illustrating that a vital aspect of human flourishing—*eudaimonia*, a life of practical wisdom—is hospitality to the strange (including, perhaps above all, "strange" perspectives) and strangers.

My claim is that hospitality in contemporary virtue ethics (which is a movement marked by a return to teleology) is an activity that we desire and do for its own sake, not for the sake of something else, and it involves what Brewer calls "unselfing." That is, forgetting about oneself, one's projects, plans, and projected expectations, and joyously surrendering to what is other than oneself: to hospitality. The paradigmatic case of this sort of "teleological hospitality" is the loving desire for another—that is, the love for another that involves full engagement in the other before oneself, to the point of time and calculation melting away. It is a full gift of the self as present, now, before (*and literally for*) the other: inching ever closer to that other in the sense of learning more, understanding more, and subsequently *loving* the other more.

The type of "dialectical" desire that Brewer has in mind is not a desire to bring about some calculated end, but rather a desire to understand and appreciate by being-with that object as fully, attentively, and hospitably as possible. The pleasure involved in being-with someone you love or doing something that you love—reading a book, hiking, dancing, having a conversation, teaching—is best described as falling into the activity at hand, to the point of being unable to think about anything other than intensifying what one is doing: to be more fully with the other, to give oneself over to the other, to act in hospitality. While this type of hospitality might sound imprudent (e.g., losing track of time, joyously surrendering without reservation), it is a vital part of human life—so vital that if we fail to engage with it, we jeopardize our ability to flourish. Beyond this, dialectical hospitality, as I interpret it, is an iteration of the metaphysical desire that Levinas has in mind, which suggests that human flourishing involves a "return" to the receptiveness that is constitutive of responsibility.

Desire and "Unselfing"

Talbot Brewer's 2009 text *The Retrieval of Ethics*[1] is without question one of the most current, original works within contemporary Aristotelian virtue ethics. One of the noteworthy aspects of Brewer's text is that it is an explicit effort to reclaim Macintyre's tasks in *After Virtue*—including its original distress about the current state of moral philosophy (6). Brewer therefore seeks to employ virtue ethics as a means of critiquing our current cultural and academic context, underscoring its fruits as capable of providing a more enduring moral scheme. And as was the case in Kant, Levinas, and Arendt, this moral scheme involves *hospitality to the strange*.[2]

Brewer's text is, as he puts it, an exercise in self-retrieval, and it contests the reigning Anglo-American conception of the self—as predominantly results-oriented, anti-contemplative, and hungry for certainty—drawing from the "conceptual scaffolding of compelling alternative pictures of the human self, its capacities, its aspirations, its concerns" (9–10). Brewer wants to paint a picture of the self that makes better sense of our lives *as we actually live them* and does not reduce us to the production-oriented, self-interested beings that the modern age has made us out to be. Like Alasdair Macintyre, Brewer stresses that unless we contest this conception of the self and *construct new values*, we will not be able to make sense of our efforts to unify our lives, based on a conception of how best to live them—that is, the "yearnings that draw us to our ideals and to each other" (8), or in the terms of this volume, *our ethico-moral yearnings to take the risk of hospitality.*

I will focus my analysis here on two crucial threads within Brewer's complex text: his notion of dialectical activity, and his notion of universal self-affirmability. The first is Brewer's response to what he understands to be an inadequate conception of human agency and its relation to desire; the second is Brewer's elucidation of the fundamental role of others within an Aristotelian ethical schema. These two threads constitute two essential aspects of what I am calling teleological hospitality: *dialectical hospitality* ("dialectical" in Brewer's sense of the term), and *dialogical hospitality*.[3]

Indirectly echoing Arendt's critique of modernity, for Brewer, the predominant conception of human agency—the "world-making" conception of agency—is that in which human action is ultimately "a species of production," the meaning of which derives from the "state of affairs [those actions] are calculated to bring about" (12). Even actions that are done for their own sake are done *so that they occur.* Under this schema, human action is always oriented toward a future state of affairs or world that they aim to bring about. The alternative to this is what Brewer calls the "evaluative outlook," with roots in the ancient and medieval Platonic and Aristotelian tradition. This outlook involves a conception of the nature of human action as always stretching toward some sense of what is good for human beings to be. This conception of human nature and action need not involve calculated production, as it includes actions that are valuable in themselves, stressing that we can be motivated without being able to identify an achievable (yet to come, expected, anticipated) state of affairs (13).

For Brewer, the "world-making" conception of agency plagues contemporary ethics, and it is especially problematic because it is insufficient in its depiction of desire and the role of practical thinking in the fulfillment of desire. This is partially due to the fact that it searches for "generic causal explanations for the events we call human actions" (13). That is, causal in the sense of one billiard ball causing another billiard ball to move—a linear transfer of energy from state A to aimed-future state B. This causal explanation of motivation misses a key aspect of what is involved in A's relation to B: the justification for (rather than causation of) B, that is, *what made the action worth doing?*[4]

It seems clear that this conception of desire is at least in some sense bankrupt, failing to adequately describe certain aspects of what it is to desire another person, or what it is to desire to fully engage in an activity. Brewer's point is that human agents have a far richer teleological structure than either spontaneity or calculation. There is a multiplicity of values one seeks to host and therefore envelop oneself in when engaging in a given activity. And while the infinite variety of reasons or values one has for engaging in something makes it seem as though our desires are "fractured into a succession of different actions," Brewer vindicates the unity involved in a given cluster of values with his notion of "dialectical activity." This term covers activities that are taken to be valuable in themselves. The "dialectical" aspect of these activities denotes the movement of digging deeper and deeper into the phenomena at hand, more fully immersing ourselves in the action by diving into the cluster of values associated with it—*unimpeded* by calculation.

The "teleological" aspect of dialectical activities refers to the sense we have of what it is to fully engage in or excel at the given activity (40), for example, getting "lost" in an amazing conversation. This is the "good sought" (*telos*), albeit not a good sought somewhere beyond the activity itself, but rather by and through intimate engagement with it, only experienced in the surrendering or forgetting of oneself and what is familiar by immersing oneself in what is otherwise than oneself. And again, this unreserved diving in—enjoying the pleasure that comes with doing something for its own sake—is nothing other than hospitality to the strange, whether that strangeness is the stranger on the other end, the unforeseeable future, or a new idea. By Brewer's account, this "attention-arresting" mode of appreciation is best characterized as "unselfing." In this intense appreciation, we are removed from all distractions, especially the "most banal and obsessive human distractions: the self" (64). This *unselfing* is dialectical hospitality, preparing us to be hosts open to uninvited and unexpected guests.

Desire so construed extends us beyond our self-concerns, as we yearn to bring the activity's intrinsic goodness into deeper focus (64)—that intrinsic goodness being (echoing Kant, Levinas, and Arendt) the stranger or the strange. Complete and utter absorption *qua* cessation of calculation is key. The pleasure involved in the loving desire for another—again, paradigmatic of the pleasure involved in any dialectical hospitality, varying only in degrees—is marked by the "mesmeric attraction," *the pull* to what is wholly present before oneself: an instance of goodness in the world that incites celebration (63). Mirroring what we saw in Levinas, the type of desire involved in dialectical activity (in Levinas's terms, metaphysical desire) is the originary hospitality that lies at the very core of our being—leading us where we want to go, without giving us any sense of where, precisely, that might be: the destination remains unknown.

With Brewer's notion of dialectical activity/dialectical hospitality in mind, we can now turn to his notion of universal self-affirmability/dialogical hospitality. Vital and unique to Brewer's retrieval of the self is his elucidation of the account of friendship that we find in Aristotle, specifically as reclamation of friendship as a necessary condition of virtue. Friendship based on the good—for Brewer, "character friendship"—is central to the good life, as it is only through character friends that we are able to develop better evaluative outlooks in life ("evaluative outlook" referring to our sense of what is *admirable*/"good" and *contemptible*/"bad," for example, immigrants should be treated with equal dignity in the United States—this is *admirable*).[5]

Thus, for Brewer, as is the case in hermeneutics (Gadamer, Ricoeur, Kearney, and company) as well as Arendt, others ultimately provide a window of insight into the way in which we understand phenomena and what the implications of those understandings might be. In isolation, we cannot see every angle. When we self-reflect, our minds tend to take the same routes, and draw the same conclusions. The role of the other is to show us aspects that are not apparent to us (we are not transparent to ourselves) and thus deepen our understanding of the outlook at hand. Others help us hone our understanding of virtue and vice—exposing vulnerabilities, blind spots, strengths, and surprising insights and connections. Dialogical hospitality is a vital occasion for honesty and creativity, bringing us to a clearer understanding of ourselves.

Beyond this, others challenge us to help ensure that our reasons and values are sound and that they are conducive to living well. It is therefore by way of character friendships that we are able to build confidence in our conception of goodness via "mutual approval of the admirable," which is a form of mutual self-awareness (242). Thus, the process of refining our ethical judgments is marked by a shift from subjective self-affirmability to universal self-affirmability—and the only way to do this is through conversation with as many character friends as possible. It is through character friendship that we *immunize* disordered thinking, unclouding our moral vision through dialogic deliberation (266). Thus, friendship is both intrinsically valuable and vital to virtue.

Dialogical hospitality is therefore crucial to moving beyond our inevitably limited perception of things—to "strange" points of view—and essential to ethical development, as this particular form of hospitality is the way in which moral outlooks come to be both shared and refined; it is the way in which common distortions in thought resulting from emotions and feelings are remedied. Proper friendship, as Brewer stresses, is grounded in *theorein*—focused contemplation on an object of understanding—in the sense that the love for other (ultimately the other's *nous*, their desire to strive toward goodness) constitutes an originary source of appreciative attention, that is, originary hospitality. It is in attending to that other that one is able to amplify the range of dialectical activities "that one can accompany and appreciate with appreciative attention" (242). Intimate relationships like these are what help us understand aspirations and admirations. Character friendships are lifelong sources of "an ethical education that tends toward outcomes that are both *eudaimonistic* and recognizably moral" (244).

For Brewer, *contra* Aristotle, character friendship does not require two completely virtuous souls, as it can occur between unequal friends insofar as the goodness is proportioned to its object. Distinct to his notion of character friendships is that they can and do evolve; they are not simply instances of static mutual admiration. Essential to character friendship is that the other has intrinsic value and is a source of appreciative attention, hospitality, unselfing. This is what differentiates character friendship from friendships based on pleasure and utility, in which the friend's value is contingent on their service of each party's respective self-interest. Character friendship uniquely involves the seemingly paradoxical self-surrender and self-affirmation—only paradoxical if we forget the hospitality housed at our core.

Character friendship, then, is constituted by dialogical hospitality, fostered by a mutual admiration of the other's sense of the good (253). Mutual admiration, ultimately facilitated by hospitality, allows each friend to give credence to the other's voice (concerned about the other's approval), and is what enables one to trust the other enough to offer one's own evaluative outlook to be inspected, scrutinized, or praised. This trust involves *not knowing* if your perspective will remain the same as it was when the conversation started, and being uncertain about where the conversation will go or what resolution (if any) might be reached. Brewer continues:

> We can assess and refine [the idiosyncratic portions] of our sensibility by dialectical alteration between expressing them in action and conversation, and interpreting the words and actions of our friends as further sources of evaluative insight. At its best, this is a mutual and continuously reiterated process, one that displaces each friend from the confines of his or her existing commitments and concerns, and permits them to discern the outlines of newly evolving concerns in the person of the other. This mutual, dialectical alteration is the process by which a distinctive, shareable sensibility comes to have a determinate and increasingly articulate form. (254)

It is, therefore, through dialogical hospitality—something that actually constitutes a very common, day-to-day occurrence—that we "attempt to deepen our understanding of the difference between the tactless and the candid, the tactful and the dishonest, the kind and the over-indulgent, the generous and the profligate, the magnanimous and the pompous, the deeply felt and the maudlin or sappy, the self-confident and the conceited, the self-respecting and the self-indulgent, the prudent and the cowardly or spineless, the brash and the rash, the accommodating and the servile" (276). These conversations unveil understanding, provide lucidity, and illuminate value.

Goodness Is Hospitality

Brewer's critique of the "world-making" conception of human agency and concomitant favoring of the "evaluative outlook" should be understood as underscoring the problem with limiting human action to instrumental motivation, as this comes at the hefty price of neglecting (if not forgetting altogether) the vital role of teleological hospitality. Brewer resurrects the significance of what is good in itself through his notion of dialectical activity, by which he retrieves the notion of goodness as intrinsic value: something deeply appreciated for its own sake, like someone we love—valuing them for no other reason than being who they are. The bottom line for Brewer, as was the case with Kant, Levinas, and Arendt, is that we are more than machines, calculators, and consumers. We are also constituted by a desire for surprise, wonder, novelty, a pull toward the experience of the strange—hospitality—which involves the joy *of letting oneself go*.

As we saw in the last chapter, the role of desire is fundamental to Levinas's account, as substitution—metaphysical desire—is the good. Goodness is precisely the desire to stretch beyond oneself as ego. *Goodness is hospitality.* Brewer's elaboration of what we find in Aristotle and Macintyre speaks to this point, and I think could be understood as exemplifying what Levinas has in mind. *Telos,* for Brewer, denotes the unimpeded immersion of oneself deeper and deeper into the appreciated activity; this unimpeded immersion of oneself in the event at hand necessarily involves the divesting of self-conscious reflection. Otherwise one would not be able to *be there,* as the process of reflection pulls one into themselves and away from their surroundings.

Brewer aptly describes this unselfing (for Levinas, the divesting of the self) as attention arresting, being riveted, utterly absorbed, engrossed, caught up in what one is doing—paying tribute to intrinsic goodness. When desiring the good, it is impossible to reflect or project—digging into memory or projecting into the future—since you are no longer a concern for yourself. Your only concern is what you are doing. There is no sense of where, specifically, that doing is headed (based on the past), no knowledge of a future state, but simply the mesmeric attraction to what you are undergoing and the desire to experience *more* of that undergoing. Based on the description that Brewer provides, paying tribute to the intrinsic goodness so clarified is precisely unhindered, unrestrained action, meaning there is no conscious fixation on a determined end outside of being-in, being-with, the activity itself. As Brewer points out, love for the other is what constitutes the original source of appreciative attention. Being enraptured by another (whether it is a friend or a lover) is paradigmatic of losing one's sense of time, one's memories, and anticipations. Love of another provides the "architecture" of dialectical desire.

This description of dialectical desire clearly resonates with Levinas's account, and Levinas goes so far as to claim that the self *is* most fundamentally *unselfing*. That is, substituting oneself for the other. Key for Levinas is that desire so construed is literally what animates us, inspires us: both in the sense of the warmth of the sun enlivening us, and in the sense of conversation delivering the urge to open up and give. Brewer's account of desire is strikingly similar to what Levinas has in mind in his depiction of substitution: the receptive movement of unselfing, divesting, dispossessing. But again, this is not something a human agent *chooses* to do, but instead it denotes the way in which we are perpetually pulled by the good, despite ourselves. *The good is an affective undergoing.* Levinas is more concerned with recovering the claim that the other has on each and every one of us—this claim being the original liberation (freedom) from reflective self-consciousness, as well as the source of all meaning whatsoever. There is a strong sense in which Levinas's project does the work of exposing the pervasiveness of unselfing, as Brewer intends to do, but for Levinas, without it, we cease to be.

With this in mind, Brewer ultimately elucidates both Aristotle's and Macintyre's teleological conception of the self in a significant way. He describes *telos* anew as the activity of giving oneself over. This does not involve seeking to bring about some further state of affairs, or calculating the means to some predetermined end, but instead involves being present to the event itself, for its own sake, desiring only to augment it (in awe), to make the experience fuller (in appreciation): to lose oneself and therefore truly host what is other. In the case of universal self-affirmability, character friends engage in conversations that seek to understand the phenomena at hand, unsure about "where" the conversation is headed. Although, as Brewer points out, moral thinking is something uniquely assigned to oneself, in relation to one's individual context, the others are vital mirrors who illuminate our blind spots and suggest new ways of understanding things. This point, while ostensibly obvious, is crucial. The other helps us habituate a hospitality to the strange, which is an essential aspect of a flourishing human life.

Echoing Aristotle, friends and moral educators are the mirrors by which we are able to observe and understand the nature of our actions. As mirrors, they disrupt our current understandings of things by asking us questions, demanding reasons, challenging us to think otherwise—that is, engaging in dialogical hospitality. Practically speaking, building character friendships is vital to *eudaimonia*. The value of virtue comes from others, and is instilled in each of us by way of conversation—be it from the stories we are told, or the conversations that help us understand new encounters, new thoughts, new feelings, or even old ones. As we saw in Kant, conversation is a vital "cultivator of virtue and a preparation for its surer practice," and the health of society hinges on conversation. It is through dialectic understood as engagement with the insights of others that we can inch ever closer to clarity; moreover, in its most complete form, friendship—the greatest of all external goods—centers on the activities of loving and activating the rational element within oneself and the other by exercising reason through dialogue. It seems clear that the habituation of conversation is essential—that is, conversation understood as hospitably opening oneself to what is other than oneself (e.g., another person's perspective), listening to phenomena, and then working to understand-*with* the other.

The important takeaway here is that to cherish something as good in itself—an essential feature of practical wisdom—future, self-interested, certain ends need to be taken off the table. This is to say that one is to act without consequences in mind, hospitable to the future that one cannot ever accurately predict. My claim is that the most essential aspect of practical wisdom so construed is that it is defined by hospitality to the unknown, a desire to host the strange and let oneself-as-ego go.

So, the question that remains is: *How do we begin, as a society, to value this sort of activity? And "return" to originary hospitality?* It seems clear that the inevitable answer is education. And more specifically, a model of education grounded in an understanding of the self as perpetually unselfing and an understanding of teaching as an important instance of character friendship working toward universal self-affirmability. With this, we can turn to question of hospitality in the classroom, exploring the pedagogical implications and applications that follow, abstracting what a pedagogy of hospitality might entail in light of the accounts presented in Part I and Part II of this volume.

8

Hospitality in the Classroom

I begin this final chapter by addressing the claim that our age, the twenty-first century in the Anglo-American West, is an age of anxiety, most tangibly in the sense that young people are more and more frequently finding themselves paralyzed in the face of the uncertain and unknown. In 2017, the *New York Times Magazine* issued an excellent feature that asked, "Why are more American teenagers than ever suffering from severe anxiety?"[1] "Severe anxiety" here refers to an inability to deal with failure (*imperfection*) to the point of being reclusive, unable to attend school, or unable to act without "certainty" about what is to come. As the article stresses, this is ultimately the result of locating value in achievement (of the future state of affairs they want to bring into existence).

The article aptly illustrates that anxiety, plaguing more than half of our undergraduates in the United States, is best defined as the overactive fight-or-flight response that perceives threats where there often are none—an overproduction of *what ifs* when standing before the future. Although we are all anxious to some degree, our culture's obsession with achievement and fulfilling self-imposed expectations has fostered an epidemic of overachieving perfectionists plagued by a crippling fear of failure—which is, more fundamentally, a fear of the pain associated with rejection and inadequacy. The article aptly describes the "crippling" dimension of anxiety as a dread that the moment of "being able to stop because you have *finally* achieved enough" will never come. That is, that one will never be enough, never be perfect.

Perfection is the enemy of "the good" in the sense that perfection—here synonymous with achieving expectations—inhibits us from straying from what we think we know is best, from going against the agenda or expectations we set for ourselves (our self-legislation), or from inadvertently arriving at new understandings. Perfection inhibits us from taking risks, which in turn inhibits us from exposing ourselves to the unexpected. The trouble that young people face today is an unwillingness to venture outside of their comfort zones, habituating a lack of resilience in the face of the unexpected, rather than the welcome of exposure, confidence before the unanticipated: that is, *an excess of hostility and a lack of hospitality*.

The Socratic Model of Learning

I will now briefly turn to my experience in pre-college philosophy to highlight several aspects of Philosophy for Kids (P4C) pedagogy that work to turn hostility into hospitality in the classroom. As I have argued elsewhere with my friend and colleague Amy Reed-Sandoval,[2] these aspects include P4Cs: (1) attempt to dismantle the more traditional "top-down" model of authority in the classroom, potentially replacing the power of the teacher with the power of the respective voices of students in the classroom; (2) emphasis on maintaining an open format that safeguards an alternative space for students to share their lived experiences/offer epistemic specificity; (3) prioritization of building a community of inquiry and fostering open collaborative conversation; and (4) commitment to promoting Socratic dialogue by insisting on active listening and humility in the classroom and on understanding and practicing philosophy as provocation.[3] For our purposes in this volume, I will specifically focus on the last item on this list, though I would contend that all four are essential to fostering a disposition of hospitality in young people.

Under the Socratic model of learning, the instructor's role is to be a present interlocutor, and, like Socrates, to hear what each student has to say and actively push their thoughts to new spaces by provoking them, by asking them *why*. It seems clear that this sort of listening is the defining feature of true conversation; active listening is what connects one's perspective to the perspective of another by *hosting* and therefore granting credence to their ideas, ultimately in hopes of working together to collectively come to new understandings. Active listening involves humility on the part of the instructor, recognizing that they, too, are a learner in the classroom, and that their students are valid sources of knowledge. This emphasis on active listening and humility calls for prioritizing inquiry and dialogue in the classroom to foster communities in which students actively participate in the co-construction of knowledge. To truly co-construct knowledge and *think together* both actively and openly, there needs to be attentive exchange among all members of the classroom, hospitality to new, different perspectives.

The other aspect of promoting hospitable dialogue in the classroom is its understanding and practice of philosophy as *provocation*. This is to say that philosophy ought to be understood as a discipline that does not hesitate to offer disquieting suggestions, that is not afraid to "offend" its participants, and that serves as an occasion to playfully bring students into the business of *knowing thyself* in all of that self's multiplicity.[4] This involves actively questioning the "politically correct" as things that "should" or "should not" be said out loud, recognizing that it can sometimes be more problematic to cover up or avoid addressing prejudices for the sake of preventing accidental "offense" than it is to offend or provoke, albeit in a hospitable way. This is one way of understanding what we propose to be an ethics of radical hospitality: educators cannot be afraid to muddy the water and complicate matters, since these complexities lend themselves to new understandings—showing us the "something more" that is not extant in our preexisting schemas.

For example, during the summer of 2017, while I was teaching a college-level Intro to Ethics course, "The Good Life," to underresourced high school students in the Mississippi Delta, I had a black student make a remark about where white people go in town, ending by saying, "No offense." I asked, "Why would I be offended?" The student was quiet. I encouraged the student to explain herself, lightheartedly asking "what" the student thought I was, and the student eventually said, "You are mixed." Somewhat shocked by how candid the conversation was—recognizing that my privilege was being made explicit—I used the student's remarks as an occasion to discuss race in relation to positions of power and socioeconomic status, lightening the conversation by letting the students work through their understanding of different stereotypes—including their impressions about me, for example, my being white enough to share in white privilege. I reminded them that philosophy as a practice works to probe stereotypes, and that generalizations always fail to capture a given phenomenon in all of its complexity.

It is important to note that I was not trying to correct the students' thinking, but was instead trying to celebrate the open/honest conversation, giving the students space to make their understandings of privilege, whiteness, and oppression manifest. The crucial takeaway from this case is that regardless of the age group, we should not hesitate to unload our presuppositions and talk about them, asking ourselves: what, if anything, are we missing? Debating "political correctness" not only warrants these conversations but also understands them as part of the process of dismantling prejudices and transcending taboos about the other—no matter *who* that other is, ultimately birthing, in radical hospitality, new perspectives. This is a concrete way in which the hospitality that would otherwise seem impossible is in fact possible by way of candid, open conversation.

The point here is that shifts in understanding—what I call "self-disruption"—are birthed from conversation, which involves listening to what is always and already most proximate to us: the stranger and the strange. Philosophy's task is to remind us that self-disruption is the work of the good. And while we cannot will shifts in our moral understanding in precisely the same way that we will ourselves to do or not do something, because it requires provocation from something *other than ourselves*, we can choose to engage in experiences that occasion narrative imagination. We can listen to others; we can converse. When I was teaching the philosophy of race and gender to high school students on the border in El Paso, Texas, one of the vibrant Latina students boldly stated, "Political correctness has gone to a whole different level. If people are all walking around on eggshells, afraid of offending anyone and everyone, how can we accomplish anything? How can we even share our opinions?" This student was ultimately expressing gratitude for our open conversation probing racial and gender-based presuppositions, understanding it as an opportunity not only to understand each other better but also to understand better the roots of our own prejudices and presuppositions.

Within philosophy in particular, especially as educators in the humanities, we can seek to instill an appreciation for goodness so construed by provoking our students, disrupting their current understandings, habituating conversation, listening to what is otherwise than certain to ourselves, no matter how uncomfortable it makes us. We can then do the same for ourselves when we get a little too cozy in our convictions, for there is always something that fails to meet the eye. To understand moral philosophy in this way—as a form of moral cultivation—is to ensure that philosophy remains the love of wisdom (*sophia*) rather than the love of knowledge (*episteme*). Instilling this sort of appreciation for self-disruption begins the process of reclaiming *courage* as a virtue: that is, courage in the sense of welcoming the strange and unknown. Moreover, instilling this sort of appreciation for self-disruption teaches us how to value, nurture, and habituate a mode of being in which the self and its preservation are not the only objects of concern. Given what we know about our anxious youth in the Anglo-American West, the time is ripe for this work.

Renewing a Common World

In her essay "The Crisis in Education," Hannah Arendt astutely points out that above all else, education is the space in which communities pay attention to newcomers—children—and decide how to prepare them to become adults and enter the community. The role of the educator is to introduce young people to the world as it is, and invite them to take responsibility for it. She writes, "The teacher's qualification consists in knowing the world and being able to instruct others about it, but his authority rests on his assumption of responsibility for that world. Vis-à-vis the child it is as though he were a representative of all adult inhabitants, pointing out the details and saying to the child: This is our world" (186). On this, she concludes:

> What concerns us all and cannot therefore be turned over to the special science of pedagogy is the relation between grown-ups and children in general or, putting it in even more general and exact terms, our attitude toward the fact of natality: the fact that we have all come into the world by being born and that this world is constantly renewed through birth. Education is the point at which we decide whether we love the world enough to assume responsibility for it and by the same token save it from the ruin which, except for renewal, except for the coming of the new and young, would be inevitable. And education, too, is where we decide whether we love our children enough not to expel them from our world and leave them to their own devices, nor to strike from their hands their chance of undertaking something new, something unforeseen by us, but to prepare them in advance for the task of renewing a common world. (193)

Echoing Arendt, we would say that hope always hangs on the new, the unexpected. And young people—the newcomers, the risk-takers (not yet weathered by the world)—play a pivotal role in exploring uncharted territory and bringing new things into being.

That in mind, it is important to ask: *What does it mean to renew a common world?* It seems clear that one answer involves fostering a disposition of hospitality—first and foremost, among young people—toward what is other: the unknown, the unanticipated, the new, the strange, the future, which inevitably involves a wager. Hospitality is the condition for the possibility of finding new common ground, and as Richard Kearney argues in Chapter 2, narrative imagination is not only the vehicle for new forms of understanding but also the necessary condition for the possibility of ethics, even though it does not *guarantee* it.[5] This insight, as Kearney illustrates in Part I, undergirds all of our work at Guestbook Project. It is when we open space for the voice of the other to be heard that we can engage in the lifelong task of learning what it means to flourish in a world with diverse others. And it is first and foremost through listening that we learn how to take responsibility for the other and ourselves—celebrating the openness that lies in our core, embracing the catharsis born in the "hostipitality" of narrative imagination, and remembering that the conversation is never finished: surprising and unimaginable understandings are forever promised, so long as we take the risk that comes with opening the door.

To end with a final pedagogical example, I want to take a moment to briefly engage Helen T. Boursier's illuminating text "The Great Exchange: An Interfaith Praxis of Absolute Hospitality for Immigrants Seeking Asylum." In it, she recounts the extraordinary practice of exchanging stories with refugees on the border of the United States and Mexico, in her words actualizing "the gift of hospitality with an unknown Other, not for oneself or for the sake of any particular religion, but for the sake of those who have lost some of their own identity as displaced persons, uninvited strangers or aliens who have no place to rest unless a nation offers hospitality."[6] Although Boursier, like René Dausner, couches the practice of hospitality as living in the image of God—and in fact praising God—it clearly resonates with much that has been discussed from a secular and more strictly philosophical perspective. What Boursier describes is a clear example of absolute or impossible hospitality *in practice*: giving for the sake of the gift, not for the sake of economic exchange.

As she depicts it, Boursier and two volunteer chaplains (along with a handful of volunteers from the San Antonio Interfaith Welcome Center) worked at an immigration detention center with the ultimate aim of bearing witness to the stranger arriving on US soil. Boursier writes, "Many of the interfaith volunteers say they acknowledge a trace of God in the refugee families who are what Richard Kearney would describe as the 'divine strangers' in our midst. Instead of viewing refugees as uninvited and unwelcome, interfaith volunteers agree with Caputo, interpreting Emmanuel Levinas's work, which would see these families as the 'trace God leaves behind when [God] withdraws from the world.'"[7]

The critical point here is that the volunteers followed what could be understood as a pedagogy of hospitality: looking beyond the totalizing categories placed on these strangers and seeing them in their uniqueness. This is of course not a classroom in the same sense as depicted earlier, but the volunteers from radically different worldviews and walks of life (some Muslim, some Jewish, others Christian) worked together to establish a safe space in which refugees—the "stateless"—are granted, above all, a voice.

That is, a safe space in which the others (most of whom were single mothers in their early twenties) are given a seat at the table, hosted in their difference, welcomed to tell their migration story—which in most cases countered prevailing narratives of why these people go through great, dangerous lengths to cross the border. The established common ground at the detention center was simply *being human*, covering all walks of life.

Returning to Kant, this practice of acting in hospitality, as Boursier outlines, stands in stark contrast to the ways in which they are received by local authorities and sent to the *hielera* or *perrera*, the freezer or the dog pen.[8] Again, these are refugees fleeing genocide. The volunteers established not only a standard of respect in their interaction but also opened spaces for creative expression—fostering *natal hospitality*, the welcome birth of the new. On this, Boursier writes:

> As a simple, yet poignant act of love, while the families hurry to get in line to confirm their bus ticket to their families scattered across the U.S., a volunteer looks each person in the eyes and simply says, "*Bienvenido*" (welcome). One volunteer said, "By the time I had greeted the last person to arrive, I could barely speak because my throat was choked with tears" (9–15–17). Joy also exploded each time the detention center ministry team facilitated art in the on-site gymnasium with 250–300 mothers and children simultaneously, and somewhat chaotically, creating art together. Art also is a joyous diversion with children at the bus station which uplifts families and volunteers.[9]

The pedagogy of hospitality that was actualized by the volunteers simply entailed selflessly giving oneself to the other, and prioritizing their needs over one's own—offering a meal, driving a family to the airport, or simply listening to what the other has to say. This in turn involved being vulnerable to and before the other, undergirded by a sense of mutual transparency. There was no hidden agenda on either end. The power of that gesture made all the difference for the immigrants seeking not only asylum, but to be treated with dignity—something that their own countries were incapable of doing. Boursier poignantly quotes Levinas: *the forgetting of the self moves justice.*[10] And she stresses that this forgetting of the self is precisely what was happening during these exchanges, proving that the seemingly impossible is in fact possible.

This point is crucial, as it underlines the very real possibility of fostering a pedagogy of radical hospitality in classrooms throughout the world, grounded in the understanding that despite real difference, we are all, similarly, members of this earth, and are all equally dignified by virtue of being human. We all belong to one world and we all deserve to be free and flourish in that freedom. While borders mark important boundaries, the same way concepts do, borders, like concepts, are porous, ever changing, ever adaptable, for this is the nature of life itself.[11]

The question, however, that remains is: What are the borders of the "we" who belong to one world? Does "we" entail the nonhumans, who are members of the earth as well? With this, we can turn to our closing remarks, including a final word on hospitality's new frontier: the nonhuman other.

Postscript
Hospitality's New Frontier: The Nonhuman Other

RICHARD KEARNEY AND
MELISSA FITZPATRICK

The call to host the stranger, open psychic and physical borders to the other, and welcome the unknown guest—advocated throughout this volume—was seriously challenged by the coronavirus pandemic. As we write the postscript to this volume in Boston in the summer of 2020, previous norms of relating to the other have been radically challenged and changed. The most basic gesture of hospitality—the handshake—has been virtually outlawed, to safeguard social distancing and prevent contagion.[1] A paradoxical suspension of hospitality for the sake of hospitality: care of the other. By contrast, hostilities toward the unknown—be it our pandemic future, economic uncertainty, respiratory failure, death, or other imponderables—are undoubtedly alive and well, exacerbated by the particularly indefinite situation that we face as a global community. Covid-19 has effectively shut down the economy both domestically and abroad, asking, if not forcing, people all over the world to shelter in place and adhere to strict social distancing guidelines when leaving the house, all while borders around the world have been closed. The rapid spread of the virus has reminded us of the difficulties that come with unconditional hospitality, as the virus itself denotes a nonhuman other *unknowingly hosted by human others*. We have been enjoined to suspend customary modes of hosting to protect public health and spare overcrowded hospitals and overworked doctors and nurses. And yet at least one poet, Kristin Flyntz, has envisaged the virus as a stranger who knocks at our door, inviting us to change our lives, daring us to accept an uninvited guest with a message for our sick and broken world. In "An Imagined Letter from Covid-19 to Humans," she conjures a mode of hospitality as "impossible" as anything conceivable :

> Stop. Just stop . . .
> Despite what you might think or feel, we are not the enemy.
> We are Messenger. We are Ally. We are a balancing force.
> We are asking you:
> To stop, to be still, to listen;
> To move beyond your individual concerns and consider the concerns of all . . .
> Many are afraid now.
> Do not demonize your fear, and also, do not let it rule you. Instead, let it speak to you—in your stillness,
> listen for its wisdom . . .
> Stop.
> Notice if you are resisting.
> Notice what you are resisting.
> Ask why.

The virus has forced us to face the difficult tensions that exist between health and economic progress, inalienable rights and global capitalism, the common good and self-interest, preparedness and paranoia. The question of what the post-pandemic future holds tests the limits of our hospitality to the unknown and the welcome disruption of our seemingly stable, though often fragile, agendas, projections, and plans.[2] In light of the fact that well over twenty million people filed for unemployment in spring 2020 in the United States alone, economic uncertainty is in many cases a matter of life or death, which is to say that the fear of not being able to put food on the table, to pay for rent, or to pay for medical expenses can quickly eclipse any fear of contracting the virus. It perhaps goes without saying that aside from medical workers, those who were most affected by the pandemic were minority communities and immigrants; and if they did not lose their jobs due to the shutdown of nonessential businesses, they were often braving the crowds as essential employees at grocery stores, pharmacies, buses, trains, and banks—leaving their respective communities with higher infection rates than more affluent suburbs.

At the heart of the pandemic, philosopher Michael Sandel posed the question: *Are we really all in this together?*—underlining the very real conflict between "meritocracy" and solidarity.[3] The virus has undoubtedly provoked new forms of hostility toward to the other. Hate-based violence found yet another occasion to rear its ugly head, the obsessive hoarding of essential goods left more vulnerable communities without them, and we were constantly reminded not to get too close, to stay six feet away from strangers, and to avoid all in-person forms of social gatherings. Thanks to technology, we were still able to connect with others from the comfort and safety of our own homes, but it would be naïve to think that this particular hostility toward what is other will not have a lasting effect on humanity.

That being said, new forms of hospitality also emerged, including but by no means limited to a more regular practice of reaching out to friends and loved ones simply for the sake of checking in, connecting, and sending gratitude; massive efforts to vindicate the stories of those affected by the virus (doctors, nurses, and survivors); an unbelievable amount of local businesses shifting all production efforts to the creation of personal protective equipment for those on the front lines, people stepping up and reaching out; and perhaps above all, a mass effort to shelter in place, wear masks, and adhere to the strict social distancing guidelines for the sake of the most vulnerable in society. While these may not be traditional instances of welcoming the stranger into one's home, they are clearly instances of prioritizing the needs of the other over oneself.

The virus dramatically reminded us just how dependent we are on others, how much our action affects those around us, and how equal we are in our vulnerability. Isolation—*being alone together*—is a clear act of hospitality to medical professionals who are putting their health on the line every day for the sake of their respective communities, as well as high-risk individuals whose immune systems would struggle to fight the disease associated with the virus. These movements of hospitality were all grounded in the crucial understanding that the well-being of the whole community is our own well-being—and vice versa. We are the other. We are all other to each other. Again, quoting Krista Tippett, while "our vulnerability and fragility before this transition is different" and in many cases unbearable, we are all transitioning, walking into the imponderable, together. Such transitions are among the most difficult things we face in life.[4] In these trying and transitory moments, humility before and hospitality to the unknown is vital, since there is only so much that we can control.

With this in mind, the challenge we are faced with is the role of discernment in understanding ourselves as hosts and the difficult balancing act between prudence and unconditional hospitality. *What if opening the door leads to disastrous if not deadly ends?* Throughout this volume, we have advocated the importance of hospitably suspending prejudices and anticipations, at the perpetual risk of being met with hostility when extending one's hand.

While we cannot know how to discern in every situation—each case being singular—we can say that one way or another, we will have occasion to encounter the new, the surprising, the strange. How we respond to those encounters makes all the difference, and it should involve undertaking the risk of understanding another's point of view. In extreme cases, this may mean that opening the door could lead to our demise, or that the other is not ready to reciprocate the gesture, not ready to listen, not ready to welcome—though we stand by the conviction that each and every one of us has tolerant and emancipatory impulses at our core. We are hosts—and we are guests. This is to say that attempting to return—and to help others return—to these impulses is never in vain, though "perfect" results are never promised, and the work is never done. Hospitality's possibilities are truly infinite and should by no means be limited to the human world.

While a full treatment of what an ethics of hospitality to nonhuman strangers might entail exceeds the scope of the current project—which has primarily focused on hospitality to the human other—we want to briefly mention how environmental *other-than-human* issues might be understood through the framework we present here. In regard to the ecological crisis itself, the facts are very clear: the climate is warming, island and coastal communities will be compromised (first), the status of displaced climate refugees (as a result of the economic activity of industrialized nations) will be a real and global problem, and the nonhuman natural world as we know it (as well as its fragile ecosystems) will deteriorate. So, the question we face is: *What role does hospitality play in all of this?* Beyond the very clear need to host climate refugees when their homes no longer exist—and to embrace them, regardless of their origin—what might it mean to host the natural world as "other"? The challenge might be raised that in regard to nature, we are in fact the ones being hosted, which is certainly true. We are guests on this earth; and nature in turn demands to be a guest in our lives whether we like it or not—reminders ranging from natural disasters and shifts in climate to diseases that know no borders. Animals, trees, and rivers are not "knocking at our door" in the same way that other people do, but they were here long before we created urban spaces and did not ask to cohabitate with urban and suburban life in the ways that they have been forced to do.

With this in mind, it seems clear that hospitality *can* work as a paradigm for ecological action, countering the way so many of us are able to hostilely look the other way in regard to environmental concerns because we are more interested in maintaining self-interested habits—not understanding ourselves as part of a fragile ecological web with the nonhuman world. This has been one of the curses of the Anthropocene. It also seems evident that letting nature be, rather than exploiting it for self-interested anthropocentric purposes (e.g., the textile industry destroying rivers with dye, or big agriculture destroying parts of the Amazon to make space for cattle fields) would require an act of hospitality in the sense of bearing witness to nature's immensity and not using it as a means to serve self-interested ends. Leaving nature alone—that is, *respecting* nature—is itself an act of hospitality that refuses hostile acts of exploitation and manipulation. Welcoming nature into our lives and letting nature welcome us back is another step yet to be taken.

The novel model of biocentrism endorses hospitality toward nature.[5] It advocates an attitude of respect for nature, that is, a moral commitment to treat *all* living organisms (human and nonhuman) as having equal inherent worth, thus extending the logic of respect for humans—acting in hospitality—to nature. This outlook notably entails an understanding of human beings as sharing a world with other organisms that are just as vulnerable as humans are. "Epidermal vulnerability" goes both ways. Beyond this, it hinges on the fact that human beings are literally constituted by other-than-human others; without other forms of life, we would cease to exist. To state the obvious, we cannot breathe without the oxygen that comes from trees in vast forests, we cannot live without fresh water, we cannot nourish ourselves without the bounties that nature provides. *I am because we are.* And the "we" here extends to more-than-human entities. We are both hosts and hostages of nature. And vice versa.

All living entities have a life force, and therefore seek to augment their own interests (e.g., a flower seeking light). This is arguably what grants their status as moral entities that have a right to be hosted as guests in a manner similar to that presented in Kant. But the bias toward human rationality's intrinsic superiority is completely arbitrary, grounded in ill-founded or unfounded prejudices; and to say that humans are better than animals is no different than saying the affluent are more valuable than the poor. (And aren't humans only more "apt" than animals in certain cases? Wouldn't a dog be better at identifying the footsteps of a missing person?) Both cases are grounded on a form of preference or taste, which is ultimately a form of self-interest. One could argue that this bias toward human superiority is an instance of an ideological Anthropocene that needs to be checked for its lack of hospitality toward what is other than our human species. With our ecological crisis in mind, conversations probing our anthropocentric biases are not only important, but, as we are repeatedly reminded, are also vital to the continuation of life on this planet. There are analogies here to interreligious hospitality in the sense of hosting different spiritual and intellectual worldviews, challenging the status quo of one's host culture and allowing it to be transformed by the foreignness of the guest (human, animal, or divine).

This is all to say that the looming ecological crisis reveals an unprecedented call for international collaboration—narrative hospitality, cooperative conversation—grounded in the understanding that, in relation to our earth, we (all of earth's diverse inhabitants) are one community. This is a call that is often met with hostility, proving that we live in an age not only of anxiety, but of divided bipartisan politics, border crises, xenophobia, ecological turmoil and global pandemics—this will certainly not be the last pandemic we experience as a global community. Which is to say that the experience of hostility toward the stranger is an undeniable part of reality for the foreseeable future. We need not understand this as ineluctable doom, however, but as a timely provocation to forge new bridges and explore uncharted understandings of *who we are, where we are going, and why.*

What we have tried to emphasize in our two-part analysis is that a "hospitable commons" can be formed only by embracing the hard work of recognizing differences, honoring the untranslatable, and relinquishing control over the limits of what can and cannot be known with mathematical certainty. Undertaking the labor of critiquing ideologies and identities, and reimagining our understanding of others and ourselves (in light of complex and painful histories) always begins by first *listening to*, and then *being willing to exchange with*, the other: the widow, the orphan, the alien, the nonhuman, or the narrative stranger we cannot even imagine. As we hope to have elucidated throughout this volume, we are who we are by virtue of hosting others, and the only way back to the self is through the other who hosts us in turn—showing us, through both word and touch, what we cannot see ourselves.

Acknowledgments

We would like to express our gratitude to the following for their kind permission to publish the visual illustrations in this volume: The Guestbook Project, the Twinsome Minds performance, and the artist, Brian Tolle, of the Irish Famine Memorial in New York City. We would also like to thank Tom Lay (acquisitions editor), Eric Newman (managing editor), Gregory McNamee (copy editor) and Jack Caputo (series editor) at Fordham University Press, whose encouragements and guidance were indispensable in the completion of this volume. Last, we are grateful to Anna Boessenkool for her invaluable assistance in proofreading and indexing the final drafts of this volume.

Notes

Introduction: Why Hospitality Now?

1. Thomas Meaney, "Who's Your Dance Partner? Europe Inside Africa," *London Review of Books* 41, no. 21 (November 9, 2019), 35–39.

2. Marina Warner, "The European Woman's Heritage," in *Visions of Europe: Conversations on the Legacy and Future of Europe*, ed. Richard Kearney (Dublin: Wolfhound Press, 1992), 41.

3. It is interesting to recall how many narratives of hospitality are brought together to form the story of a people. Biblical Israel, for example, is asked to remember its stories of hosting strangers, for they too have been strangers in exodus, aliens wandering in the desert in search of a home (Gn 18–19). The people of "Israel," as Paul Ricoeur notes, came to be through "narrative hospitality"—recollecting stories of oppression, salvation, and care for the "widow, the orphan and the stranger." That is what is meant by the "people of the book." There would be no Israel if there had not been this historical memory and reenactment of narrative hospitality (John Cavanaugh-O'Keefe, *Strangers: 21 Claims in the Old Testament*, 2016). And the same might be said about other Abrahamic cultures—no Christianity without the narratives and parables of the Gospels, no Islam without the Koran and Haddith. Or, regarding non-Abrahamic religions, no Hinduism without the Upanishads and Bhagavad Gita; no Buddhism without the stories of the Buddha, Bodhisattvas, and Dalai Lamas. See *Hosting the Stranger: Between Religions*, ed Richard Kearney and James Taylor (New York: Continuum, 2011). See here also the Zen ideal of the relationship among equals as a mutual exchange and circulation of the roles of host and guest (*Hinju Gokan*). The contemporary

Zen philosopher Ueda Shizuteru writes that "the free exchange of the role of host is the very core of dialogue." Cited in Bret David, "Zen's Non-egocentric Perspectivism," in *Buddhist Philosophy: A Comparative Approach*, ed. Steven Emmanuel (Chichester: Wiley-Blackwell, 2018), 123–143. On the notion of narrative identity and religions of the book, see Paul Ricoeur, "Conclusions" to *Time and Narrative*, vol. 3 (1990). On the question of narrative hospitality in relation to works of collective commemoration, see our discussions in Chapter 3.

4. Hence the felicitous polyvalence of the term "host" in Eucharistic communion, meaning the one who feeds, the one who is fed and the bread itself. Even in the hospitality parlance of a restaurateur, the host of the house offers a *table d'hôte* to the guest client (also called *hôte*). We shall return to this double sensibility of hosting-guesting.

5. The same might be said for Anglo-American philosophy, where hospitality gets little or no explicit treatment until some recent retrievals of Aristotelian virtue ethics and post-Kantian reflections on perpetual peace. And even in such recent retrievals—discussed in Chapter 7—it is never the central theme, treated on its own terms for its own sake, but rather in service of other questions governing the discourse within applied ethics. In the two parts of this volume, we endeavor to render explicit the underlying concerns with hospitality in the thought of Levinas, Ricoeur, and Derrida—bringing each into conversation with the other while offering a brief hint of a second conversation between these key continental philosophers and recent pioneering thinkers in Anglo-American ethics. We intend this latter dialogical hint as a small gesture of philosophical hospitality.

6. Marcel Mauss, *The Gift* (New York: Routledge, 1990). Of the "potlatch" as primal exchange of gifts between rival tribes he writes: "Only then did people learn how to create mutual interests, giving mutual satisfaction, and, in the end, to defend them without having to resort to arms. Thus, the clans, the tribes and peoples have learnt how to oppose and to give to one another without sacrificing themselves to one another. This is what tomorrow, in our so-called civilized world, classes and nations and individuals also, must learn" (106). See also Lewis Hyde, *The Gift* (New York: Vintage Books, 1979), and João J. Miranda Vila-Chã (editor), O Dom, a Verdade, e a Morte: Abordagens e Perspectivas / The Gift, Truth, and Death: Approaches and Perspectives. Special edition of *Revista Portuguesa de Filosofia* 65 (2009).

7. See Jacques Derrida: "For there to be gift, it is necessary that the gift not even appear, that it not be perceived or received as gift," in *Given Time* (Chicago: University of Chicago Press, 1992), 16. See also Derrida, *The Gift of Death* (Chicago: University of Chicago Press, 1995).

8. Marcel Hénaff, *The Philosophers' Gift: Reexamining Reciprocity* (New York: Fordham University Press, 2019).

9. Dausner draws here on the research by contemporary thinkers like Dan Bulley and Alex Balch.

10. René Dausner, "Humanity and Hospitality: An Approach in the Times of Migration," *The Religious and Ethnic Future of Europe/Scripta Instituti Donneriani Aboensis* 28 (2018): 51–67, at 53.

11. Ibid., 54.

12. Ibid. See also Jacques Derrida, "Hospitality, Justice and Responsibility: A Dialogue with Jacques Derrida," and John Caputo, "Reason, History and a Little Madness: Towards an Ethics of the Kingdom," both in *Questioning Ethics*, ed. Richard Kearney and Mark Dooley (New York: Routledge, 1998), 65–104; and John Caputo, *The Insistence of God: A Theology of Perhaps* (Bloomington: Indiana University Press, 2013).

13. Quoting Dausner, "Hospitality that deserves to be called hospitality had to be unconditional and even more: impossible. Impossibility is being defined by hospitality because hospitality is more and different to just rule, law and order. . . . We are obliged to be hospitable even if we do not know—and perhaps never will know—what hospitality is. Hospitality in this sense has to be impossible because if it were possible we would have nothing to decide. A possible hospitality would mean that we follow the rights and politics of hospitality as a machine, not as a human being. Derrida is convinced that only the impossibility of hospitality could open a space for the other. The impossibility does not simply mean a non-possibility but rather the search for an unknown, necessarily innovative form of hospitality that is open to a new world to come" ("Humanity and Hospitality," 56). For a discussion of Derrida's "messianicity," see "Derrida's Mystical Atheism," in *The Trace of God: Derrida and Religion*, ed. Edward Baring and Peter Gordon (New York: Routledge, 2014).

14. See Peter Block, Walter Brueggemann, and John McKnight, *An Other Kingdom: Departing the Consumer Culture* (Hoboken, NJ: Wiley, 2016). The commons is the natural and cultural body of resources accessible to all members of a society, including natural materials such as air, water, and a habitable earth. These resources are held in common by all members of human society, not owned privately or available for private economic speculation, investment, or exploitation. We are indebted to Richard Rohr for introducing us to this discussion of the gift economy. See also the discussion of a "commons of the body" in Richard Kearney, *Touch: Recovering Our Most Vital Sense* (New York: Columbia University Press, 2021).

15. Lynn Twist and Teresa Barker, *The Soul of Money: Transforming Your Relationship with Money and Life* (New York: Norton 2017), 74–75. Twist elaborates the implications of this ethic of hospitality and sufficiency for a converted attitude toward wealth: "Grounded in sufficiency, money's movement in and out of our life feels natural. We can see that flow as healthy and true, and allow that movement instead of being anxious about it or hoarding. In sufficiency, we recognize and celebrate money's power for good—*our* power to do good with it—and we can experience fulfillment in directing the flow toward our highest ideals and commitments. When we perceive the world as one in which there is enough and we are enough to make the world work for

everyone everywhere. With no one left out, our money carries that energy and generates relationships and partnerships in which everyone feels able and valued, regardless of their economic circumstances" (103, 119). This alternative ethical approach to money invites us to convert fetishistic commodities back into real material goods, refusing the division into spirit and matter—a binary division between superstructure and infrastructure that serves the capitalist model of segregation and value-free accumulation and concentration of wealth for the few over the many. See also here Charles Eisenstein, *Sacred Economies: Money, Gift and Society in an Age of Transition*: (Berkeley: North Atlantic Books, 2011) "Part of the healing that a sacred economy represents is the healing of the divide we have created between spirit and matter. In keeping with the sacredness of all things, I advocate an embrace, not an eschewing of materialism. I think we will love things more and not less. We will treasure our material possessions, honor where they came from and where they will go. . . . The cheapness of our things is part of their devaluation, casting us into a cheap world where everything is generic and expendable . . . the essential need that goes unmet is the need for the sacred—the experience of uniqueness and connectedness" (27–28). The purpose of a sacred economy of gift and hospitality is not to "prattle on about angels, spirit and God" but to treat "relationship, circulation and material life itself as sacred" (426). Cited and commented by Richard Rohr, "Making Do with More: Economy Old and New" (in Daily Meditations blog, Center for Action and Contemplation) November 25, 2019, cac.org/making-do-with-more-2019-11-25.

16. See Richard Rohr, *Moral Capitalism*" (in Daily Meditations, Center for Action and Contemplation) November 27, 2019, cac.org/moral-capitalism-2019-11-27) (2019) and Arthur Simon, *How Much Is Enough? Hungering for God in an Affluent Culture* (Grand Rapids, MI: Baker Books, 2003).

17. See respected evolutionary biologist Elisabet Sahtouris's claim that nature fosters collaboration and reciprocity over mere competition and survival (cited in Rohr, Daily Meditations). See similar arguments by theologian Catherine Keller in her dialogue with the new physics, *Cloud of the Impossible: Negative Theology and Planetary Entanglement* (New York: Columbia University Press, 2014); *Intercarnations* (New York: Fordham University Press, 2017); and *Political Theology of the Earth* (New York: Columbia University Press, 2018).

18. Lindsay Balfour, *Hospitality in a Time of Terror: Strangers at the Gate* (Lewisburg, PA: Bucknell University Press, 2018).

19. See the illuminating phenomenological analysis of Edward Casey, "Strangers Gate," in *Phenomenologies of the Stranger: Between Hostility and Hospitality*, ed. Richard Kearney (New York: Fordham University Press, 2010), 39–48.

20. Balfour, *Hospitality in a Time of Terror.*

21. *On Being with Krista Tippett* (podcast), "How to Love a Country," November 27, 2019.

22. Ibid.

23. In his recent book *Our Wild Calling: How Connecting with Animals Can Transform Our Lives—and Save Theirs* (Chapel Hill, NC: Algonquin Books,

2019), Richard Louv describes many persuasive examples of how humans and animals can connect, host, and heal each other. "In the habitat of the heart—in that whisper of recognition between two beings when time seems to stop, when space assumes a different shape—in that moment, we sense a shared soul. That is what connects the woman and the bear, the diver and the octopus, the dog and the child, the boy and the jaguar, the fisherman and the golden eagles on the shore" (273). Louv makes a passionate plea for human reconnection with our tangible world of living nature. Noting our growing Nature Deficit Disorder and the dramatic decline of thousands of animal and plant species—between 1970 and 2014 the global wildlife population shrank by 60 percent (World Wildlife Fund statistics)—Louv appeals to what he calls a "habit of the heart," which he argues needs to be revived if our world is to survive. He cites various ecopsychological studies about how proximity to trees and animal-assisted therapies can greatly reduce symptoms of illness and augment our sense of well-being—"having a profoundly positive impact on our health, our spirit and our sense of inclusiveness in the world" (3). While digital and gaming technology (e.g., the 2016 online game *No Man's Sky*) can generate countless new "virtual species" and invite us to take bold leaps of creative imagination, Louv argues that we also need to take action in our physical world to bring us back into touch with our ontological guests on this planet—our animal and natural "strangers." He writes that "reversing or slowing biodiversity collapse and climate change cannot be accomplished solely through science, technology, or politics." That is necessary but not sufficient. "Success will require a far larger constituency than what exists today, one with greater emotional and spiritual connection to the family of animals, recognizing in all nature the 'inescapable network of mutuality' that Martin Luther King Jr. called for among human beings" (3). In the name of this principle of mutual hospitality, Louv advocates an advance toward the "Symbiocene": an age of connectedness beyond excarnation, "encompassing reciprocity and redistribution, where wildness survives, albeit in newer forms and in unexpected places, where we live in balance with other life" (272). We would argue that such connectedness demands an "ethics of hospitality" based on what Louv calls the "reciprocity principle," whose first steps are these: "For every moment of healing that humans receive from another creature, humans will provide an equal moment of healing for that animal and its kin. For every dollar we spend on classroom technology, we will spend at least another dollar creating chances for children to connect deeply with another animal, plant or person. For every day of loneliness we endure, we'll spend a day in communion with the life around us until the loneliness passes away" (273).

1. Linguistic Hospitality: The Risk of Translation

1. Paul Ricoeur, *On Translation*, trans. Eileen Brennan (London: Routledge, 2006), 23. Earlier versions of material in the first part of this essay were published in the following: "Introduction" to ibid.; "'Linguistic Hospitality'—

The Risk of Translation," *Research in Phenomenology* 49 (2019); and "Double Hospitality—Between Word and Touch," *Journal for Continental Philosophy of Religion* 1 (2019): 71–89.

2. Ricoeur, *On Translation*.

3. Ibid. See also the detailed hermeneutic analysis of James Taylor, "Translation as a Model for Hospitality," in *Hosting the Stranger*, ed. Richard Kearney and James Taylor (New York: Continuum, 2011), 11–23.

4. Emile Benveniste, *Le vocabulaire des institutions indo-européenes* (Paris: Éditions de Minuit, 1968).

5. Antoine Berman, *L'épreuve de l'étranger* (Paris: Gallimard, 1984).

6. Julia Kristeva, *Strangers to Ourselves* (New York: Columbia University Press, 1991).

7. Jacques Derrida, *Of Hospitality* (Paris: Galilée, 2000), 77.

8. Derrida mentions these terms in "On the Gift: A Discussion between Jacques Derrida and Jean-Luc Marion Moderated by Richard Kearney," in *God, The Gift and Postmodernism*, ed. John Caputo and Michael Scanlon (Bloomington: Indiana University Press, 1999), 130–137.

9. Paul Ricoeur, "Epilogue: Difficult Pardon," in *Memory, History and Forgetting* (Chicago: University of Chicago Press, 2009).

2. Narrative Hospitality: Three Pedagogical Experiments

1. Paul Ricoeur, "Reflections on a New Ethos for Europe," *Philosophy & Social Criticism* 21, nos. 5–6 (1995): 3–13, at 7; republished in *Paul Ricoeur: A Hermeneutics of Action*, ed. Richard Kearney (London: Sage, 1996).

2. Ibid., 8.

3. Ibid., 9.

4. Richard Kearney, "Memory and Forgetting in Irish Culture," in *Recovering Memory: Irish Representations of Past and Present* (Cambridge: Cambridge Scholars Publishing, 2007), 148–150.

5. Note the discussion of the role of touch and the handshake in the Postscript and in Chapter 4 herein. See also Richard Kearney, "Double Hospitality: Between Word and Touch," *Journal of the Continental Philosophy of Religion* 1, no. 1 (2019): 71–89.

6. Tom Epstein, ed., "On Hosting the Stranger," special issue of *New Arcadia Review* 4 (2010); Chris Yates, ed., "Hospitality: Imagining the Stranger," special issue of *Religion and the Arts* 14–15 (2011); Richard Kearney and James Taylor, eds., *Hosting the Stranger: Between Religions* (New York: Continuum, 2010); Richard Kearney and Eileen Rizo-Patron, eds., *Traversing the Heart: Journeys of Inter-Religious Imagination* (Leiden: Brill, 2010); Richard Kearney and Kascha Semonovitch, eds., *Phenomenologies of the Stranger: Between Hostility and Hospitality* (New York: Fordham University Press, 2011). Our present volume may be seen, in many respects, as a fifth publication in this series of ongoing conversations.

7. On my debt to my three Paris mentors—Ricoeur, Derrida, and Levinas—see Richard Kearney, "'Where I Speak From': A Short Intellectual Autobiography," in *Debating Otherness with Richard Kearney: Perspectives from South Africa*, ed. Yolande Steenkamp and Danie Veldsman (Johannesburg: AOSIS, 2018). See Chapter 1 herein, which reprises the analysis of the Ricoeur/Derrida/Levinas debate on hospitality researched in my earlier essays, "Linguistic Hospitality—The Risk of Translation," *Research in Phenomenology* 49 (2019): 1–8, and "Double Hospitality," *Journal for Continental Philosophy of Religion* 1 (2019): 71–89. The Guestbook project has been especially guided by the hermeneutics of narrative exchange expounded by Paul Ricoeur in "Reflections on a new Ethos for Europe"/"Quel éthos pour l'Europe?" in *Imaginer l'Europe*, ed. P. Koslowski (Paris: Éditions du Cerf, 1992), 107–118.

8. See Richard Kearney, "Be the Difference," in *Be the Change*, ed. Maurice Sweeney (Dublin: Drombeg Books, 2015). See also the video version of this story on guestbookproject.org.

9. I am indebted to my good friend Ronan Sheehan, the writer, for reminding me of the importance of this story.

10. Kearney, "Where I Speak From."

11. See the Guestbook documentaries on Syrian and Afghan refugees, *Between Two Islands*, by Angelos Bougas (2018), and on Mexican immigrants, *Under a Sheltering Sun*, by Clay Venetis on guestbookproject.org. See also here related works on interconfessional hospitality by Helen Boursier, *The Ethics of Hospitality: An Interfaith Response to US Immigration Policies*, in *The Great Exchange: An Interfaith Praxis of Absolute Hospitality for Immigrants Seeking Asylum—The Meaning of My Neighbor's Faith*, ed. Alexander Y. Hwang and Laura E. Alexander (Lanham, MD: Lexington Books, 2019). These works document and explore an interfaith project of hospitality for immigrants seeking asylum in the United States from the violence in their Central American homelands, primarily the Northern Triangle of Guatemala, El Salvador, and Honduras. The argument is situated in conversation with arts-based research that emerged from a pastoral care ministry inside an immigrant family detention facility and includes qualitative research with interfaith volunteers who have assisted asylum seekers. More on this in the final chapter.

12. See Freud, "Mourning and Melancholy," and Ricoeur's "Memory and Forgetting" in *Questioning Ethics*, ed. Richard Kearney and Mark Dooley (London: Routledge, 1998). Such work, we argue, involves a difficult process of therapeutic anamnesis—always mindful that "amnesty is never amnesia."

13. Seamus Heaney, *The Redress of Poetry* (New York: Farrar, Straus and Giroux, 2011), 200. I have developed this analysis of dual and multiple belonging in Richard Kearney, *Postnationalist Ireland* (New York: Routledge, 1997).

14. See Richard Kearney and Sheila Gallagher, *Twinsome Minds: An Act of Double Remembrance* (Cork: Cork University Press, 2017). See also my expanded critical analysis of these themes in "The Ethics of Narrative Remembrance" in

Richard Kearney and Mark Dooley, eds., *Questioning Ethics: Contemporary Debates in Philosophy* (New York: Routledge, 1999), 18–33; Richard Kearney, "Memory in Irish Culture," in *Memory Ireland*, ed. Oona Frawley (Syracuse, NY: Syracuse University Press, 2014), 3:138–151; and Michael D. Higgins, "Reflection on the Gorta Mór: The Great Irish Famine," in *When Ideas Matter: Speeches for an Ethical Republic* (London: Zeus Head, 2016), 54–74.

15. See my development of this idea of the Fifth Province in the analysis of the Irish Famine Memorial later in this chapter.

16. James Joyce, *Finnegans Wake*, book 3, Chapter I (New York: Viking Press, 1939), 403.

17. For the full text of our "Twinsome Minds" experiment in narrative hospitality, see Kearney and Gallagher, *Twinsome Minds*. But if the writers of Ireland offered a particularly cathartic response to the traumas of 1916, this is by no means a uniquely Irish experience. I think it is no accident that one the most powerful testimonies to the traumas of apartheid—*Country of My Skull*—was written by a South African poet, Antjie Krog. Here, too, poetry and art represent powerful forms of narrative healing and hospitality. I am also reminded of Atom Egoyan's extraordinary testament to the trauma of the Armenian genocide in his film *Ararat* as well as countless authors, artists, and filmmakers who have kept the memory of the holocaust alive—Amos Oz, Paul Celan, Milena, Etty Hillesum, Claude Lanzmann, Stephen Spielberg, Art Spiegelman, and many more—all observing Primo Levi's plea to "keep retelling the story of Auschwitz so that it can never happen again." But we must also honor Adorno's question—"after Auschwitz who can write poetry?"—acknowledging the limits of narrative catharsis. Is not speechlessness sometimes the most appropriate response to horror? And yet one cannot deny the indefatigable call of healing. It does not go away. History needs story to combine emotional affect with cognitive understanding—the double power of catharsis—in order to bring the past back to life again, so that we can "feel what wretches feel," empathize with the pain of the persecuted, and be struck by the terror of it all. Or, to repeat the lesson of Aristotle's *Poetics*: we often need a narrative plot (*muthos mimesis*) to reconfigure past sufferings into a meaningful act of affective catharsis: an imaginative revisiting of our innermost "passions" (*pathemata*) of "pity and fear." Otherwise there would be no purgation, no reckoning, no release—just a bare chronicle of facts: irresistible fatality. Story and history need each other for unspeakable wounds to become visible scars: for past pain to be felt and embraced. For archive to become art, cathartic healing must be a matter of both knowing *and* feeling, of body as well as mind, of being touched as well as being informed. I return to this point in Chapter 4. For a further development of these themes see Richard Kearney, "A Hermeneutics of Wounds," and Elizabeth Corpt, "Encountering the Psychoanalyst's Suffering: discussion of Kearney's 'A Hermeneutics of Wounds,'" both in *Unconscious Incarnations: Psychoanalytic and Philosophical Perspectives on the Body*, ed. Brian Becker,

John Panteleimon Mannousaki, and David M. Goodman (New York: Routledge, 2018).

18. Ricoeur, "Reflections on a New Ethos for Europe."

19. These ethical difficulties find cogent critical articulation in ways of remembering the Holocaust. See Elizabeth Ann Ellsworth, "The U. S. Holocaust Museum as a Scene of Pedagogical Address," *Symploke* 10 (2002): 13–31; Caroline Wiedmer, *The Claims of Memory: Representations of the Holocaust in Contemporary Germany and France* (Ithaca, NY: Cornell University Press, 1999); Tony Judt, *Postwar* (New York: Penguin, 2005).

20. Paul Ricoeur, *La mémoire, l'histoire, l'oubli* (Paris: Éditions du Seuil, 2000), 82ff.

21. See Julia Kristeva's reading of uncanny homelessness in *Strangers to Ourselves* (New York: Columbia University Press, 1991).

22. Declan Kiberd, *Inventing Ireland* (London: Vintage Books, 1996); Luke Gibbons, *Transformations in Irish Culture* (Cork: Cork University Press, 1996); and R. F. Foster, *The Irish Story: Telling Tales and Making It Up in Ireland* (London: Penguin Press, 2001), 23ff.

23. This sense of spatial and temporal invention is compounded by the fact that the roofless cottage remains unrestored and is exposed to local Manhattan weather. Unlike most works of art, this installation is half construct and half nature—an artificially contrived synthesis of "real" stone and soil and architectural-sculptural design. The underground tumuli and passageways, by which one enters the cottage from beneath, are further reminders that the cottage has a dark buried history, recalling not only the Neolithic Irish burial chambers of Newgrange in County Meath but also the unmarked mass graves of thousands of famine victims in Ireland and elsewhere. The fact that these subterranean passageways are themselves paneled with glass panes covered in various texts and subtexts—historical, political, fictional, rhetorical, spiritual, apologetic, testimonial—further adds to the sense of a plurality of voices. Tolle's memorial refuses to yield a quick fix. There is no single, assured access to this placeless place, this timeless time, this homeless host. It cannot be "naturalized" as a literal recovery of a landscape. Yet it cannot be explained away either as a purely "aestheticized" sculpture residing in some museum space—for the site alters continually with the surrounding climate, one season covered with weeds, potato shoots, and wildflowers, another with snow or mud; and at all times registering the odors, reflections, shadows, and sounds of the city. We are thus palpably reminded of the passing of time, of historical transience that no monumental fixation can bring to a stop. The myth of an eternal Celtic landscape is demystified before our very eyes. Tolle's installation epitomizes a hospitality to the stranger and the strange.

Not that there were not efforts by certain officials to propagate familiar myths. On opening the site, for example, Governor Pataki of New York spoke of the opportunity offered here "to touch the sod of our heritage," while Mayor Giuliani concluded his inaugural speech with the words, "May this beautiful

Memorial, like Ireland itself, be forever free, forever green." And some members of the Irish Tourist Board praised the installation's capacity to evoke "the rolling hills of old Ireland," conveniently forgetting that the quaint potato field is planted over a slab of concrete and surrounded by high rises. Certain Irish American groups were also quick to contribute their dime of rhetorical nostalgia. Even the Irish government weighed in, at one point offering an authentic "stone" from every county in Ireland (thirty-two in all, along with an ancient pilgrim standing stone). While Tolle initially resisted such sentimental appropriations, he soon came to acknowledge that these readings should not be dismissed as ineligible. Instead he realized that any *interactive* installation of this kind must learn to incorporate many opposing views into the process of the work itself as an open text of interpretation. It should rather serve as a site of unconditional hospitality, hosting multiple and even contradictory perspectives. Tolle decided, accordingly, to accommodate the wish of many visitors to relocate the old counties of Ireland by accepting the stones and then placing them at random throughout the landscape. The rocks scattered throughout the site served to reiterate the role of those in the walls and lintels of the cottage itself—that is, to function as "indices" for the lost bearings of forgotten dwellers rather than as "icons" of an original presence.

24. Sigmund Freud, "Mourning and Melancholy," in *The Pelican Freud Library* (London: Penguin, 1984), 2:251–268.

25. Robin Lydenberg captures this radically hermeneutical sense of Tolle's design in her essay "From Icon to Index: Some Contemporary Visions of the Irish Stone Cottage," in *Eire/land*, ed. Vera Kreilkamp (Boston: McMullen Museum of Art, Boston College, 2003), 127–133. Her analysis is worth quoting at length:

> Tolle designed the memorial to invite and incorporate the viewer's active engagement with the land and its history rather than with vague nostalgia or the iconography of fixed and sentimentalized stereotypes. One entrance into the memorial leads visitors through an underground passageway up into the ruined cottage. . . . The walls of the passageway are constructed of alternating sedimented bands of stone and frosted glass on which official and unofficial testimonies from those who experienced the Famine are cast in shadows. This sculptured layering evokes the geologically and historically sedimentary aspect of the Irish landscape. Hunger is not naturalized or aestheticized here but contextualized historically and politically, giving forceful articulation, for example, to the failure of British officials to alleviate massive starvation. Entering the quarter acre of Ireland through this buried history, viewers cannot simply delight in the landscape as idealized icon: the cottage interior is cramped and exposed, the "rolling hills" are the remnants of uncultivated potato furrows. Visitors may enter the installation by stepping directly onto the sloping earth and climbing up through the landscape to the ruined

cottage and its prospect; there they discover, belatedly, the textual history buried below. Whether the memorial is entered from above or from below, the charm of the landscape and its violent history exist in productive tension. (131)

For a further development of this theme see Richard Kearney, "Exchanging Memories; New York Famine Memorial," in *Navigations: Collected Irish Essays 1976–2006* (Syracuse, NY: Syracuse Press, 2006), 310–320.

26. See "The Fifth Province," in Kearney, *Postnationalist Ireland*, 99–100.

27. Lydenberg, "From Icon to Index," 132.

28. As Lydenberg writes: "This memorial makes no claim to enlighten visitors with a totalizing narrative of the Irish Famine; the texts create a mixture of facts, political propaganda, and personal experience—the imaginative work of fantasy, desire, and hope. Tolle's design offers a transitional passageway through fragmented, often anonymous, voices in the embedded texts and an accompanying audio collage, both of which will be revised, updated and expanded periodically in response to continuing crises in world hunger. The narrative is discontinuous, full of gaps and silences; Tolle teases out multiple meanings by placing fragments in shifting juxtapositions rather than in fixed narrative sequence. A heritage industry presentation of history as a recoverable and repeatable past to be fixed 'like a fly in amber' is displaced here by . . . a 'preposterous history' that multiplies uncertainty and doubt. This alternative mode of history calls for an alternative mode of memorial, one that would . . . defy easy readability and consumer satisfaction to communicate instead dissatisfaction, complexity, and a sense of loss." Ibid., 131.

29. One might, indeed, even extend the scope of intertextual allusion to include the fictional famine testimonials of writers like Tomas O'Flaherty and Tom Murphy, or of filmmakers like Scorsese whose representation of Irish emigrant warfare in the *Gangs of New York* reminds us that within earshot of Battery Park stood the Five Points: the notorious battleground where fixated memories of vengeance and obsession played themselves out in bloody conflict in the 1860s—Nativists and Hibernians locked in hatred, impervious to the work of mourning, catharsis, and forgiveness.

30. See Jacques Derrida, *Specters of Marx* (New York: Routledge, 1994) and *On Cosmopolitanism and Forgiveness* (New York: Routledge, 2001). For a contrasting view of the tension between the hermeneutic and deconstructive takes on forgiveness and violence, see the epilogue of Paul Ricoeur's *Memory, History and Forgetting*, trans. David Pellauer (University of Chicago Press, 2005), entitled "Difficult Pardon."

31. Ricoeur, "Reflections on a New Ethos," 7.

32. Hans-Georg Gadamer, *Truth and Method* (London: Sheed & Ward, 1975).

33. Ricoeur, "Reflections on a New Ethos," 7.

34. Ibid., 8.

35. Ibid., 9.

36. Ibid., 8: "the past is not only what is bygone—that which has taken place and can no longer be changed—it also lives in the memory thanks to arrows of futurity which have not been fired or whose trajectory has been interrupted." I am thinking here also of Jurgen Habermas's reading of the European enlightenment as an "unfinished project of modernity."

37. Ibid.

38. Ibid., 9.

39. Ibid, 11.

40. I am thinking here of Daniel Cohn-Bendit's famous rallying cry of solidarity in 1968: *"Nous sommes tous des Juifs allemands."* And also of the identification of the Choctaw Nation with Irish famine victims in 1847 expressed in a generous donation—a gesture of mutual empathy repaid by Ireland to the Choctaws during the coronavirus pandemic of 2020. One must be careful in such transnational gestures, of course, to avoid a blanket rhetorical positing of "sameness" that could perpetrate another kind of violence by assuming someone else's historical trauma as one's own. If indifference is one enemy of commemoration, too easy appropriation is another. Good memory seeks the middle way between an overly dispassionate distance and facile overidentification.

3. Confessional Hospitality: Translating across Faith Cultures

1. Paul Ricoeur, "Reflections on a New Ethos for Europe," *Philosophy & Social Criticism* 21, nos. 5–6 (1995): 3–13, at 12–13.

2. See my analysis of Christian and Abrahamic narratives of hospitality in Richard Kearney, *Anatheism* (New York: Columbia University Press, 2010), Part I. See also the extraordinary research work of Claudio Monge, *Dieu hôte: Recherche historique et théologique sur les rituels de l'hospitalité* (Paris: Zeta Books, 2008).

3. Ibid., 13.

4. Ibid., 10.

5. Ibid., 6–7. See also Marianne Moyaert's excellent discussion of this subject in *Ritual Participation and Interreligious Dialogue*, ed. Marianne Moyaert and Joris Geldhof (New York: Bloomsbury, 2016), and her essay "The (Un)translatability of Religions? Ricoeur's Linguistic Hospitality as Model for Interreligious Dialogue," *Exchange* 37 (2008): 337–364.

6. Jürgen Habermas and Jacques Derrida, *Philosophy in a Time of Terror: Dialogues with Jürgen Habermas and Jacques Derrida*, ed. Giovanna Borradori (Chicago: University of Chicago Press, 2003), 55ff. See also Hent de Vries and L. E. Sullivan, *Political Theologies: Public Religions in a Post-Secular World* (New York: Fordham University Press, 2006), a volume showing how perilous the political takeover of religion has become. I am grateful to Lovisa Bergdahl for many of these references: see her "Lost in Translation: On the Untranslatable and Its Ethical Implications for Religious Pluralism," paper read at the SCPR Conference at Gordon College, Wenham, Massachusetts, 2008. For a longer

version of this discussion of the Habermas-Derrida debate, see Kearney, *Anatheism*, 172ff.

7. See my study of responses to 9/11 in "On Terror," in *Strangers, Gods and Monsters* (London: Routledge, 2002), 109–139.

8. Samuel Huntington, *The Clash of Civilizations and the Remaking of the World Order* (New York: Simon & Schuster, 2003), 21. I am grateful to Donatien Cicura for this reference in *Identity and Historicity in African Philosophy*:

> According to Huntington, the process of creating enemies is an inherent component of the process of being a self, of acquiring or appropriating an identity. Identity is made of allies (those who belong to my group) and enemies (those with whom I complete either individually or as a member of a group). In this line of thought, Huntington's idea of identity is analogous to the interpretation Francis Fukuyama gave of Plato's *thumos* in *The End of History and the Last Man* (New York: Penguin, 2002). Human beings identify themselves in thyumotic terms, that is, they need self-esteem, recognition and approbation. To this extent, conflict with an enemy reinforces the above qualities in a group, and procures comfort and a sense of gratification.

As Huntington himself puts it: "The need of individuals for self-esteem leads them to believe that their group is better than other groups. Their sense of self rises and falls . . . with the extent to which other people are excluded from their group." Samuel Huntington, *Who Are We? The Challenge to America's National Identity* (New York: Simon & Schuster, 2004), 25. For recent critiques of this adversarial model of politics and religion, see Amartya Sen, *Identity and Violence* (New York: Norton, 2007); Homi Bhaba, *The Location of Culture* (New York: Routledge, 1994); Martha Nussbaum, *For Love of Country* (Boston: Beacon, 2002); and Kearney, *Strangers, Gods and Monsters*, 23–40.

9. Habermas and Derrida, *Philosophy in a Time of Terror*, 55.

10. Habermas, "Religion in the Public Sphere," *European Journal of Philosophy* 14, no. 4 (2006): 6.

11. Habermas and Derrida, *Philosophy in a Time of Terror*, 55.

12. Habermas, "Religion in the Public Sphere," 9–10.

13. Ibid., 18.

14. Ibid., 10.

15. Habermas, "A Conversation about God and the World," in *Religion and Rationality: Essays on Reason, God and Modernity*, ed. Eduardo Mendieta (Oxford: Blackwell, 2000), 148–149.

16. Ibid. On the need for a complementary rational dialogue between secular and religious citizens, see Jürgen Habermas and Joseph Ratzinger, *The Dialectics of Secularization* (San Francisco: Ignatius Press, 2006), 43–47.

17. Habermas cited by Lovisa Bergdahl, "Lost in Translation," 3–4. I am very grateful to Bergdahl for bringing these arguments and texts to my attention.

18. See Walter Benjamin, "The Task of the Translator," in *Illuminations* (New York: Harcourt Brace Jovanovich, 1973), and Jacques Derrida, *The Ear of the Other: Otobiography, Transference, Translation* (New York: Schocken Books, 1985).

19. Habermas, "Religion in the Public Sphere," 10–12; also in *Between Naturalism and Religion* (Cambridge: Polity Press, 2006), cited and commented on by Bergdahl, "Lost in Translation," 3.

20. Benjamin, "The Task of the Translator," 70. On the limits of interreligious translatability as both a possibility and impossibility of symmetrical dialogue, see Catherine Cornille, *The Im-Possibility of Religious Dialogue* (New York: Herder & Herder, 2008). See also Edith Stein in *On The Problem of Empathy* (in the *Collected Works of Edith Stein, Vol 3*, Washington, DC: ICS Publishers, 1989), where she talks about our phenomenological encounter with the other as a "primordial experience of the non-primordial," that is, as a direct experience of the indirectness of the "stranger" within every person we encounter, be they familiar or foreign. On this theme, see also Max Scheler, *The Nature of Sympathy* (London: Taylor & Francis, 2017) and Derrida's discussion of the elusive, irreducible Other in Husserl's Fifth *Cartesian Meditation* in "Hospitality, Justice and Responsibility," in *Questioning Ethics*, ed. R. Kearney and Mark Dooley (London: Routledge, 1999), 66–83.

21. Benjamin, "The Task of the Translator," 75, 81.

22. See Julia Kristeva's analysis of these themes in *Strangers to Ourselves* (New York: Columbia University Press, 1991).

4. Carnal Hospitality: Gesturing beyond Apartheid

1. See Richard Kearney, "Memory and Forgetting in Irish Culture," in *Recovering Memory: Irish Representations of Past and Present*, ed. Irene Gilsenan Nordin, Hedda Friberg, and Lene Yding Pedersen (Cambridge: Cambridge Scholars Publishing, 2007), 148–150.

2. Marina Warner, "The European Woman's Heritage," in *Visions of Europe*, ed. Richard Kearney (Dublin: Wolfhound Press/RTE, 1992).

3. I discuss these biblical and political examples in detail in the first chapter of my book *Touch: Recovering Our Most Vital Sense* (New York: Columbia University Press, 2021).

4. See the development of these arguments in ibid., ch. 2, "Philosophies of Touch: From Aristotle to Phenomenology."

5. Pumla Gobodo-Madikizela, *A Human Being Died That Night: A South African Woman Confronts the Legacy of Apartheid* (New York: Houghton Mifflin, 2003), 6. I am greatly indebted to Robert Vosloo's illuminating essay for many of the citations and references below, "Touch Gives Rise to Thought: Paul Ricoeur and Pumla Gobodo-Madikizela on Dealing with the Past, Mutual Recognition and Embodied Performativity," in *Debating Otherness with Richard Kearney: Perspectives from South Africa*, ed. Daniël Veldsman and Yolande Steenkamp (Durbanville: AOSIS Publishing, 2018).

6. Gobodo-Madikizela, *A Human Being Died That Night*, 13.
7. Ibid., 14–15.
8. Ibid., 15.
9. See Ricoeur, *Memory, History, Forgetting*, 489–493.
10. Gobodo-Madikizela, "Remorse, Forgiveness, and Rehumanization: Stories from South Africa," *Journal of Humanistic Psychology* 42, no. 1 (2002): 7–32.
11. Ibid., 19–20.
12. Ibid., 20.
13. Gobodo-Madikizela, *A Human Being Died That Night*, 32.
14. Ibid.
15. Ibid., 33.
16. Ibid., 39.
17. Ibid., 42. For a similar act of "impossible" pardon, see the moving account of Eric Lomax's meeting with his former torturer in a Japanese prisoner-of-war camp in *The Railway Man: A POW's Searing Account of War, Brutality, and Forgiveness* (New York: Norton, 1995).
18. Gobodo-Madikizela, *A Human Being Died That Night*, 39.
19. Ibid., 67–68. See our previous analyses of decisive carnal encounters with the stranger/other/enemy in *Carnal Hermeneutics*, ed. Richard Kearney and Brian Treanor (New York: Fordham University Press, 2015); *Phenomenologies of the Stranger*, ed. Richard Kearney and Kascha Semonovitch (New York: Fordham University Press, 2011); and Richard Kearney, *Strangers, Gods and Monsters* (New York: Routledge, 2003).
20. Gobodo-Madikizela, *A Human Being Died That Night*, 98–99.
21. Gobodo-Madikizela, "Trauma, Forgiveness and the Witnessing Dance," *Journal of Analytical Psychology* 53, no. 2 (2008): 169–188, at 176–177.
22. Gobodo-Madikizela, *Dare We Hope? Facing Our Past to Find a New Future* (Cape Town: Tafelberg, 2014), 1, 35. One might ask here why a similar miracle of remorse and empathy did not occur between SS officer Adolph Eichmann and his benign jailer, Captain Less, around the Holocaust trial in Jerusalem, documented by Hannah Arendt in *Eichmann in Jerusalem*.
23. Antjie Krog, *Country of My Skull: Guilt, Sorrow, and the Limits of Forgiveness in the New South Africa* (New York: Broadway Books, 2000), 30.
24. See the further development of this kind of embodied knowing in *Carnal Hermeneutics* and the more detailed analysis of this question in *Touch*, chs. 1 and 4.
25. Variations on handshakes in different national cultures are found in the "Concluding Remarks" to this chapter. I am grateful to my students Tian Kang and Urwa Haweed for their research on this subject and to my colleague and friend Marianne Moyaert for her helpful exchange on this subject at the "Religion and Violence" conference, University of Vienna, April 2018.
26. Such a hermeneutics of touch is evidenced in the earliest stories of wisdom traditions—Euryclea touching Odysseus's scar, Thomas touching Christ's wound, Adam touching Yahweh's hand (depicted by Michelangelo)

See also here Jean-Luc Nancy's suggestion in *Noli Me Tangere* (New York: Fordham University Press, 2008) that Jesus's final meeting with Mary Magdalene was not a total absence of touch (certain paintings show Mary brushing Christ's garments or skin with her hand) but rather a warning not to "grasp" or "possess"—in other words, not to hang on to Jesus but to allow him to be other, a passing stranger (*hospes*), so she can be liberated into the inclusive love of the disciples. There are many ways of touching the hands of gods and men—as we know from Michelangelo's Sistine Chapel—just as there are different ways of shaking hands with the devil. Carnal hermeneutics is about trying to know the differences. For more on these and other examples see Kearney, *Touch*, ch. 3, "Wounded Healers."

27. I am grateful to my Boston College student Tian Kang for his description of the Chinese traditional salute:

> Due to the shared Confucian philosophy of the group, traditionally people do not greet each other (or show their trust) by shaking hands, hugging or kissing, because they want to avoid physical contact (which was considered impolite since feudal times). Instead they bow with "folded hands" (作揖, *zuo yi*), holding a fist with the right hand and putting the left over it. As people normally use their right hand to hold weapons, to fight and to kill, the right hand was reckoned as "the hand of death," and the left was, on the contrary, "the hand of life." Thus, the withholding gesture indicates the suppression of violence. In fact, the Chinese character for 'martial' is 武 (*wu*), is signified by putting 止 (*zhi*, which means 'to stop') and 戈 (*ge*, which means 'spear') together. This dialectic of force and prevention of force would have been, for most Chinese, more complicated than the simple gesture showing one's trustworthiness by extending a bare hand for the counterpart to shake.

28. I am grateful to Urwa Hameed for these examples, offered at a Guestbook international conference in Vis, Croatia, on June 30, 2019. She also provided an interesting example of the Islamic code of hospitality in Pakistani and Indian culture. She spoke of a very small city in Pakistan called Multan, made up of several small agrarian towns with a hot climate, which served as a residential spot for many large-scale landlords. The trend of migration toward the cities has diminished this characteristic marking those villages, but it can still be felt in many ways. Often, due to land conflict, shortage of water, internal family tensions, wounded honor, or other reasons, feuds developed between rival landlords that could extend to bloodshed. But even then, if a person knocked on the door of the other, they felt it their obligation to open the door, welcome the enemy, treat them with every luxury they could afford, and protect their life even at the expense of their own as long as they were a "guest" in the house. Once the person had left, the enmity and hatred could ensue for generations, but at the moment the person is a guest, the host will sacrifice his or her own life to save him/her. There was a specific example in which the son of a rival

landlord asked for refuge in the house of the other family because he was followed by a group of men who were seeking to kill him. The host landlord gave refuge to the son of the enemy and sent his twenty-four-year-old son outside to deal with the robbers. The landlord's son ended up losing his life in the attempt. There were no feelings of regret even after the death, only pride and satisfaction that they were able to properly host the guest to the extent they possibly could. Also in most Celtic cultures, hospitality was traditionally considered an absolute sacred duty and command (*Geis*) which hosts felt toward their guests. See the story of Cuchulainn in Anne Bernard Kearney, *Lovers, Queens and Strangers* (Dublin: A and A Farmer, 1999).

29. See the analysis of this phenomenon of diacritical spacing in Richard Kearney, "Ecrire la chair: L'expression diacritique chez Merleau-Ponty," *Chiasmi International* 15 (Fall 2013): 21–35.

5. Hospitality beyond Borders: The Case of Kant

1. Richard Kearney, "Hospitality: Possible or Impossible," *Hospitality and Society* 5, nos. 2–3 (2013): 173–184.

2. Robin May Schott, "Kant and Arendt on Hospitality," *Jahrbuch für Recht und Ethik/Annual Review of Law and Ethics* 17 (2009): 183–194, at 185–186.

3. Kant takes pains to distinguish this (the World Republic's constitution) from the constitution belonging to a state of nations, noting that a state requires superiors (the legislators) and inferiors (the legislated), setting up power dynamics that will inevitably inhibit the efforts of the constitution. It is important to note that nations enter into a league of nations, suggesting that it will be a union of nations, rather than a universal monarchy (which Kant thinks is impossible anyway, given the vast variety of languages and religions).

4. Because practical reason does not involve describing reality (as is the case with speculative reason in the *First Critique*), but determining it, Kant finds it more effective to start with a priori principles. Pure practical reason "proves its reality and that of its concepts by what it does," thus giving us insight into the (a priori) idea of freedom (5:3). Further paraphrasing Kant in the Preface to the second *Critique*: With speculative reason, we had to begin with the senses and end with principles, but will proceed in the reverse order with practical reason, because we are considering reason in relation to the will (and its causality). Here (in the process of the critique of practical reason), the law of causality from freedom—that is, from our practical rational principle—constitutes the unavoidable beginning and determines the objects to which alone it can be referred (5:5–14).

5. For an innovative phenomenological account of moral sensibility in Kant, especially the exalting dimension of experiencing the moral law, see Owen Wares, "Kant on Moral Sensibility and Moral Motivation," *Journal of the History of Philosophy* 52, no. 4 (October 2014): 727–746. Wares's account is comprehensive and has without question influenced my own interpretation.

6. Here I have in mind Anti-Climacus's notoriously difficult description of the self at the beginning of Kierkegaard's *The Sickness Unto Death*, ed. and

trans. Howard V. Hong and Edna H. Hong (Princeton: Princeton University Press, 1980), 14.

7. This point is underscored beautifully by Hannah Arendt in *The Human Condition* (Chicago: University of Chicago Press, 1958) in Part IV on *Action*, in which she explicitly pays homage to Kant's notion of freedom, recast as *natality*. I will return to this point in the next chapter.

8. See Kant's *Metaphysics of Morals* in *Practical Philosophy* (Cambridge: Cambridge University Press, 1996).

9. In Kierkegaard, this experience manifests itself as anxiety: the potentially painful possibility of letting go of what is not in one's control (outcomes in the future) juxtaposed with a desire to act in way that will lead to pleasantly anticipated consequences. In his *Lectures on Ethics*, Kant describes this perceived tension as that between the two motives to action in man: "the one—self-love—is derived from himself, and the other—the love of humanity—is derived from others and is the moral motive." *Lectures on Ethics*, trans. Louis Infield (New York: Harper & Row, 1963), 200. I think we could also describe the tension as that between war and peace, hostility and hospitality. He continues, "if the purposes of self-love did not demand our attention, we would love the other and promote their happiness" (201). Kant stresses that the unity and harmony of our mental powers can feel at times like a pursuit to gain victory over oneself, but it is far better not to need to gain victory over ourselves, i.e., not to be at war (144, 4).

10. Schott, "Kant and Arendt on Hospitality," 183–187.

6. Impossible Hospitality: From Levinas to Arendt

1. James Mensch, *Levinas's Existential Analytic: A Commentary on Totality and Infinity* (Evanston, IL: Northwestern University Press, 2015), 19–20.

2. To "totalize" the other is to encapsulate them into a presumed category or concept (e.g., X is a racist).

3. I am grateful to an anonymous reader of an earlier version of this chapter for pointing out the trouble with using the word "ontological" in relation to Levinas, given his sweeping critique of (Heideggerian) ontology. I use the term here to stress that Levinas is ultimately providing a transcendental account of what it is to be (answering the question, What is reality?). The trouble, however, with understanding Levinas's work as ontological suggests that if ethics is reality, then ethics (that is, an ethics of hospitality) is automatic, which, *ontically* speaking, is clearly not the case. The point I hope to make clear here is that even if a *response* to the other is not necessary, the other has always already claimed me. It is true Levinas takes issue with ontology (as trapped in the realm of essence, cognition, reflection, consciousness), but he is reclaiming ethics as first philosophy (metaphysics), which has something to do with reality/being/existence itself (as otherwise than essence). That being said, I will use the terms ontology and ontological somewhat interchangeably with metaphysics and metaphysical with this explanation in mind.

4. For Levinas, *consciousness* denotes an understanding of cognition that involves perceiving, intending, intuiting concepts or essences, and offering them to retention (memory) and protention (anticipation of the future). Consciousness is the process by which we thematize phenomena, and store those themes for ourselves for future use. This can be understood as theoretical reason, reflection, introspection, discursive reasoning, speculative reason, and so on. I will use these terms somewhat interchangeably to signify the conceptual mode of knowing that relies on memory and expectation.

5. This term is taken from her fantastic entry on Levinas in the *Stanford Encyclopedia of Philosophy*.

6. Kant notoriously states, "Thoughts without content are empty; intuitions without concepts are blind" (A51/B76). Levinas is contesting precisely this point, stressing that this there is a gnosis that is otherwise than perception, intentionality, and conscious identity. Levinas is describing what it is to intend an object that exceeds our intentions: a nonspatial, nontemporal, noncognitive content, that is, the infinite. It is the encounter with something offering more than we can formulate in our intentions, requiring us to readjust our interpretation, or understanding, over and over again.

7. See Chapter 4, and also Richard Kearney, *Touch: Recovering Our Most Vital Sense* (New York: Columbia University Press, 2021), Chapter 2, as well as the section on Levinas in "What Is Carnal Hermeneutics?" in *Carnal Hermeneutics*, ed. Richard Kearney and Brian Treanor (New York: Fordham University Press, 2015).

8. Judith Butler, "Precarious Life, Vulnerability, and the Ethics of Cohabitation," *Journal of Speculative Philosophy* 26, no. 2 (2012): 134–151. A crucial (and Levinasian) point that Butler makes in this article is that consent is not a sufficient ground for delimiting the global obligations that form our responsibility. Quoting Butler, "responsibility may well be implicated in a vast domain of the nonconsensual" (141).

9. That is, to be this particular set of flesh and bones.

10. As Levinas writes, "Enjoyment is the very production of a being that is born, that breaks the tranquil eternity of its seminal or uterine existence to enclose itself in a person, who in the living world is at home with itself." *Totality and Infinity: An Essay on Exteriority*, trans. Alphonso Lingis (Pittsburgh: Duquesne University Press, 1969), 147.

11. It is important to point out that Kant's tweak in the B-edition of the first *Critique* involves him making this precise point, albeit by arguing for a relation of dependency between our a priori intuitions (space and time) in his refutation of psychological idealism (which is ultimately an attempt to prove the objective reality of outer intuition). As Kant writes,

> However harmless idealism may be considered in respect of the essential aims of metaphysicians, it still remains a scandal to philosophy and to human reason in general that the existence of things outside us (from

which we derive the whole material of knowledge, even for our inner sense) must be accepted merely on faith, and that if anyone thinks good to doubt their existence, we are unable to counter his doubts by any satisfactory proof. . . . This consciousness of my existence in time is bound up in the way of identity with the consciousness of a relation to something outside me, and it is therefore experience not invention, sense not imagination, which inseparably connects this outside something with my inner sense. For outer sense is already in itself a relation of intuition of something actual outside of me, and the reality of outer sense, in its distinction from the imagination, rests simply on that which is here found to take place, namely, its being inseparably bound up with inner experience, as the condition of its possibility. . . . But though intellectual consciousness does indeed come first, the inner intuition, in which my existence can alone be determined, is sensible and is bound up with the condition of time. This determination, however, and therefore the inner experience itself, depends upon something permanent, which is not in me, and consequently can be only something outside me, to which I must regard myself as standing in relation. The reality of outer sense is necessarily bound up with inner sense, if experience in general is to be possible at all. (B xl).

Key for Kant is that inner experience is conditioned by outer experience, so even though the only thing we can be "sure" about is inner experience (time), this is ultimately determined by what is outside of myself. Kant's thesis is that the mere, but empirically determined, consciousness of my own existence proves the existence of objects in space outside of me (space denoting permanence, time-determination) (B276).

12. Levinas tips his hat to Kant by noting that the Copernican revolution's crucial insight is that being is determined on the basis of sense (Kant's Transcendental Aesthetic), rather than sense being determined on the basis of being. *Otherwise Than Being or Beyond Essence*, trans. Alphonso Lingis (Pittsburgh: Duquesne University Press, 2011), 129.

13. For a very clear account of how Kant's "conditional" hospitality fits into the Derrida/Ricoeur/Kearney debate, see René Dausner, "Humanity and Hospitality: An Approach in the Times of Migration," *The Religious and Ethnic Future of Europe/Scripta Instituti Donneriani Aboensis* 28 (2018): 51–67.)

14. Butler, "Precarious Life," 137.

15. Arendt, too, doubts if recognizing the rights to have rights is really possible (see *Origins of Totalitarianism*, Orlando, FL: Harcourt Books, 1968, at 267–302). As she puts it, as quoted by Robin May Schott, "humanity, which for the eighteenth century, in Kantian terminology, was no more than a regulative idea, has today become an inescapable fact. This new situation, in which "humanity" has in effect assumed the role formerly ascribed to nature or history, would mean in this context that the right to have rights, or the right

of every individual to belong to humanity, should be guaranteed by humanity itself. It is by no means certain whether this is possible." "Kant and Arendt on Hospitality," *Jahrbuch für Recht und Ethik/Annual Review of Law and Ethics* 17 (2009): 183–194, at 187. Schott, pulling from Seyla Benhabib, does a brilliant job outlining the resonances and differences between Arendt and Kant in relation to a global order (without nationality, humanity is abstract and empty), and the various ways in which Arendt's position is marked by paradox. For Arendt, national rights ought to involve guarantees for strangers beyond domestic borders (190).

16. Ibid., 191.

17. Ibid., 188.

18. The quote is taken from Arendt's 1954 text "The Crisis in Education," in *Between Past and Future* (New York: Penguin, 1968), 170–193, at 185.

19. See both the *Origins of Totalitarianism* and "We Refugees" (in *The Jewish Writings* [New York: Schocken Books, 2007], 264–274) for her response to the problem of statelessness and her discussion about each human being's inalienable right to have rights (preserved regardless of one's legal status in a given state). She is especially concerned about the conflation of human rights with legal-national rights.

20. Note that this is not Arendt's term.

21. Schott, "Kant and Arendt on Hospitality," 191. As Schott underlines, for Arendt, hospitality and right do not go together hand in hand as neatly as Kant would have it; hospitality does not "replace the rights and obligations of national citizenship."

22. Ibid., 192.

23. Hannah Arendt, "Thinking and Moral Considerations," in *Responsibility and Judgment* (New York: Schocken Books, 2003), 159–189, at 165–168.

24. Allen Speight, "Arendt on Narrative Theory and Practice," *College Literature* 38, no. 1 (Winter 2011): 115–130. It perhaps goes without saying that Arendt's understanding of narrative influenced Ricoeur's own narrative theory.

25. Ibid.

26. Arendt, "Thinking and Moral Considerations,"163.

7. Teleological Hospitality: The Case of Contemporary Virtue Ethics

1. Talbot Brewer, *The Retrieval of Ethics* (Oxford: Oxford University Press, 2009).

2. Through Brewer himself does not use the term "hospitality," it seems clear that, phenomenologically speaking, what he thinks constitutes a flourishing human life necessarily involves what we have been describing here as the wager of hospitality over hostility.

3. Note that these terms are not Brewer's.

4. By Brewer's account, the world-making view limits the subject to a form of desire that represents attitudes toward propositions—for example, I will go

dancing Friday night—and that these sorts of desires are guided by the "direction of fit" between the world and the proposition's object of desire: that I bring it about that I go dancing on Friday night (14). This explanation for action can always be traced back to a belief in the world or state of affairs that one desires to bring about: the preapproved proposition, inhospitable to anything outside of that proposition.

5. In Brewer's terms, an evaluative outlook is "a person's characteristic sense of the evaluative features of actual or possible human doings" (244). An evaluative outlook is *subjectively* self-affirming when the subject is able to approve of the outlook at hand (i.e., when we are okay with what that outlook is suggesting to us); an evaluative outlook is *interpersonally* self-affirming if at least two people are able to approve of the outlook at hand; and an evaluative outlook is universally self-affirming if it affirms "all possible embodiments of the same outlook, whether in its possessor or in others" (244). For instance, the evaluative outlook that children should be forced to work at age ten might have subjective or interpersonal self-affirmability, but it clearly lacks universal self-affirmability. Evaluative outlooks lacking universal self-affirmability warrant extensive conversation, so as to hash out whether or not the view in mind really warrants admiration or approval—and *why*.

8. Hospitality in the Classroom

1. For more, see Benoit Denizet-Lewis, "Why Are More American Teenagers Than Ever Suffering from Severe Anxiety?" *New York Times Magazine*, October 11, 2017.

2. See Melissa Fitzpatrick and Amy Reed-Sandoval, "Race, Pre-College Philosophy, and the Quest for a Critical Race Pedagogy in Higher Education," *Ethics and Education* 13, no. 1 (2018): 105–122. I am paraphrasing key portions of that article here and repeating some of the anecdotal evidence.

3. Ibid., 12–13.

4. In "Teaching Our Children Well," as well as elsewhere, Claire Katz underscores the centrality of the Delphic order "know thyself" in the project of philosophy—philosophy's "original, powerful aim" (531)—and describes the way in which the discipline has suffered in the decentering of that order, including its loss of interest in education. Katz, "Teaching Our Children Well: Pedagogy, Religion and the Future of Philosophy," *Crosscurrents* (Winter 2004): 530–545. See her *Levinas and the Crisis of Humanism* (Bloomington: Indiana University Press, 2013) to get a sense of her robust Levinasian solution.

5. Richard Kearney, "Narrative Imagination: Between Ethics and Poetics," in *Philosophy and Social Critique* 21, nos. 5–6 (1995): 173–190.

6. Helen T. Boursier, "The Great Exchange: An Interfaith Praxis of Absolute Hospitality for Immigrants Seeking Asylum," in *The Meaning of My Neighbor's Faith: Interreligious Reflections on Immigration*, ed. Alexander Y. Hwang and Laura E. Alexander (Lanham, MD: Lexington Books, 2019), 133–147.

7. Ibid., 5.

8. Ibid., 8.
9. Ibid., 10.
10. Ibid., 15.

11. To discuss briefly another pedagogical example of this activity in the classroom: as we saw in the discussion of "narrative hospitality" in Chapter 2, Guestbook Project operates on the maxim "*if someone asks you who you are, you tell your story.*" Overcoming violence and facilitating conflict resolution involve precisely this: expressing your own story and listening to the story of the other. Guestbook's Storybites initiative aims to create a participatory space for people who want to share stories that highlight a radical or surprising shift in their perspective through the encounter with another person. One of my especially liberal students in an environmental ethics class that I taught at Boston College submitted a Storybite sharing her then-recent experience of hosting a radically different perspective while doing service work near the Appalachian Mountains in "coal-mining country" in Kentucky. She describes a conversation that she had with a struggling coal miner, suffering from Lou Gehrig's disease, who hospitably welcomed her into his home. Given the temper of the time, just before the 2016 election, the conversation shifted to politics and the question of coal mining in America, despite the pressure of climate change and the need to reduce fossil fuel emissions. Sarah explains that she felt hostile toward him for ignoring the ecological crisis, but as he explained that coal mining was his livelihood and that his livelihood—literally his ability to survive—depended on his industry surviving, she could not help but see his predicament. This is to say that the man's hospitality *qua* openness and honesty—partially motivated by Sarah's willingness, as guest, to host his perspective in turn—helped Sarah understand the more complex picture, and, to be clear, not to negate her point of view, but to allow *the different* to help her amplify and augment it. She simply did not have the same concerns that he did, and she truly struggled to see the coal-mining industry as anything but problematic (which it is)—and certainly not a source of anyone's livelihood (which it also is). And, how could she? She does not live in a region where coal mining is a fundamental part of the local economy. "Impossibly" choosing hospitality beyond political borders and engaging in dialogical hospitality augmented Sarah's understanding of reality, allowing her to see something she not only had never seen before, but could not even imagine. Sarah's story is one among a plethora of others depicting the importance of laboring to understand, rather than insisting on being understood; hosting the strange by relinquishing control over what one believes to *certainly* be the case (assuming infallibility); and reminding ourselves that there is always something more than meets the eye, and we are able to grow only when we have the courage to explore uncharted territory, dive into strange waters, even at the risk of modifying our original, cherished convictions, but always with the promise of augmenting our current understanding of things. (See http://guestbookproject.org/storybites/ for examples from students in Egypt, Croatia, South Africa, and elsewhere.) In Sarah's case, this does not

mean that she will suddenly start denying the importance of reducing fossil fuel emissions, ignoring the very real ecological crisis, or advocating for the coal-mining industry. These positions are objectively problematic. Echoing the transformative moment depicted in Richard Kearney's example of dramatic narrative exchange between ex-paramilitary prisoners in Northern Ireland, it means that in choosing hospitality over hostility—listening to the other, refusing to see the other as "evil"—Sarah is able to understand something about the stranger that renders them human, like herself. It is ultimately through dialogical hospitality that she is able to better understand the "borders" of her own perspective, and to acknowledge different and foreign ways of understanding as vehicles to exploring and reimagining what it means to coexist in a civil fashion with others—and creatively facilitate precisely that.

Postscript. Hospitality's New Frontier: The Nonhuman Other

1. See Richard Kearney, "Coda on Covid-19," in *Touch: Recovering Our Most Vital Sense* (New York: Columbia University Press, 2021), 133–140. See also Tim Teenan, "Coronavirus Has Killed the Power of Touch. How Do We Reconnect?" *Daily Beast*, April 16, 2020.

2. See John Manoussakis, "Coronations: Notes from the Quarantine," *The New Polis*, April 10, 2020.

3. Michael Sandel, "Are We All in This Together?" *New York Times*, April 13, 2020. See also Kearney, "Coda on Covid-19."

4. *On Being with Krista Tippett* (podcast), "Living the Questions: How Can I Find My Footing in a Shifting World?" April 14, 2020. See also Julia Kristeva, "*L'humanité redécouvre la solitude existentielle, le sens des limites et la mortalité*," *Corriere del Sera*, March 29, 2020.

5. Paul Taylor, "The Ethics of Respect for Nature," *Environmental Ethics* 3, no. 3 (1981): 197–218.

Bibliography

Arendt, Hannah. *Between Past and Future*. New York: Penguin, 1968.
———. *Eichmann in Jerusalem*. New York: Viking Press, 1963.
———. *The Human Condition*. Chicago: University of Chicago Press, 1958.
———. *The Jewish Writings*. New York: Schocken Books, 2007.
———. *The Origins of Totalitarianism*. Orlando, FL: Harcourt Books, 1968.
———. *Responsibility and Judgment*. New York: Schocken Books, 2003.
Balfour, Lindsay. *Hospitality in a Time of Terror: Strangers at the Gate*. Lewisburg, PA: Bucknell University Press, 2018.
Baring, Edward, and Peter E. Gordon. *The Trace of God: Derrida and Religion*. New York: Routledge, 2014.
Becker, Brian, John Panteleimon Mannousaki, and David M. Goodman. *Unconscious Incarnations: Psychoanalytic and Philosophical Perspectives on the Body*. New York: Routledge, 2018.
Benjamin, Walter. "The Task of the Translator." In *Illuminations*, 69–82. New York: Harcourt Brace Jovanovich, 1973.
Benveniste, Émile. *Le vocabulaire des institutions indo-européenes*. Paris: Éditions de Minuit, 1968.
Bergdahl, Lovisa. "Lost in Translation: On the Untranslatable and Its Ethical Implications for Religious Pluralism." Paper read at the Society for Continental Philosophy and Theology Conference at Gordon College, Wenham, Massachusetts, 2008.
Bergo, Bettina. "Ontology, Transcendence, and Immanence in Emmanuel Levinas's Philosophy." *Research in Phenomenology* 35 (2005): 141–179.
Berman, Antoine. *L'épreuve de l'étranger*. Paris: Gallimard, 1984.

Bhaba, Homi. *The Location of Culture*. New York: Routledge, 1994.
Block, Peter, Walter Brueggemann, and John McKnight. *An Other Kingdom: Departing the Consumer Culture*. Hoboken, NJ: Wiley, 2016.
Boursier, Helen T. "The Great Exchange: An Interfaith Praxis of Absolute Hospitality for Immigrants Seeking Asylum." In *The Meaning of My Neighbor's Faith: Interreligious Reflections on Immigration*, edited by Alexander Y. Hwang and Laura E. Alexander, 133–147. Lanham, MD: Lexington Books, 2019.
Brewer, Talbot. *The Retrieval of Ethics*. Oxford: Oxford University Press, 2009.
Butler, Judith. "Precarious Life, Vulnerability, and the Ethics of Cohabitation." *Journal of Speculative Philosophy* 26, no. 2 (2012): 134–151.
Camus, Albert. "The Myth of Sisyphus." In *Basic Writings in Existentialism*, edited by Gordon Marino, 489–492. New York: Modern Library, 2004.
Caputo, John D. *The Insistence of God: A Theology of Perhaps*. Bloomington: Indiana University Press, 2013.
Caputo, John, and Michael Scanlon. *God, The Gift, and Postmodernism*. Bloomington: Indiana University Press, 1999.
Cavanaugh-O'Keefe, John. *Strangers: 21 Claims in the Old Testament*. Self-published, 2016.
Claviez, Thomas. *The Conditions of Hospitality: Ethics, Politics, and Aesthetics on the Threshold of the Possible*. New York: Fordham University Press, 2013.
Cornille, Catherine. *The Im-Possibility of Interreligious Dialogue*. New York: Herder & Herder, 2008.
Corpt, Elisabeth. "Encountering the Psychoanalyst's Suffering: Discussion of Kearney's 'A Hermeneutics of Wounds.'" In *Unconscious Incarnations*, edited by Brian Becker et al., 43–49. New York: Routledge, 2018.
Dausner, René. "Humanity and Hospitality: An Approach in the Times of Migration." *The Religious and Ethnic Future of Europe/Scripta Instituti Donneriani Aboensis* 28 (2018): 51–67.
David, Bret. "Zen's Non-egocentric Perspectivism." In *Buddhist Philosophy: A Comparative Approach*, edited by Steven Emmanuel, 123–143. Chichester: Wiley-Blackwell, 2018.
Denizet-Lewis, Benoit. "Why Are More American Teenagers Than Ever Suffering from Severe Anxiety?" *New York Times Magazine*, October 11, 2017.
Derrida, Jacques. *The Ear of the Other: Otobiography, Transference, Translation*. New York: Schocken Books, 1985.
———. *The Gift of Death*. Chicago: University of Chicago Press, 1995.
———. *Given Time*. Chicago: University of Chicago Press, 1992.
———. *Of Hospitality*. Paris: Galilée, 2000.
———. *On Cosmopolitanism and Forgiveness*. New York: Routledge, 2001.
———. *Specters of Marx*. New York: Routledge, 1994.
de Vries, Hent and Sullivan, L. E. *Political Theologies: Public Religions in a Post-Secular World*. New York: Fordham University Press, 2006.
Eisenstein, Charles. *Sacred Economies: Money, Gift and Society in an Age of Transition*. Berkeley: North Atlantic Books, 2011.

Ellsworth, Elizabeth Ann. "The U.S. Holocaust Museum as a Scene of Pedagogical Address." *Symploke* 10 (2002): 13–31.

Fitzpatrick, Melissa, and Amy Reed-Sandoval. "Race, Pre-College Philosophy, and the Quest for a Critical Race Pedagogy in Higher Education." *Ethics and Education* 13, no. 1 (2018): 105–122.

Foster, R. F. *The Irish Story: Telling Tales and Making It Up in Ireland*. London: Allen Lane, 2001.

Freud, Sigmund. "Mourning and Melancholy." In *The Pelican Freud Library*, 2: 251–268. London: Penguin, 1984.

Frodeman, Robert, and Adam Briggle. "When Philosophy Lost Its Way." *New York Times*, January 11, 2016.

Gadamer, Hans-Georg. *Truth and Method*. London: Sheed & Ward, 1975.

Gibbons, Luke. *Transformations in Irish Culture*. Cork: Cork University Press, 1996.

Gobodo-Madikizela, Pumla. *Dare We Hope? Facing Our Past to Find a New Future*. Cape Town: Tafelberg, 2014.

———. *A Human Being Died That Night: A South African Woman Confronts the Legacy of Apartheid*. New York: Houghton Mifflin, 2003.

———. "Remorse, Forgiveness, and Rehumanization: Stories from South Africa." *Journal of Humanistic Psychology* 42, no. 1 (2002): 7–32.

———. "Trauma, Forgiveness and the Witnessing Dance." *Journal of Analytical Psychology* 53, no. 2 (2008): 169–188.

Guenther, Lisa. *The Gift of the Other: Levinas and the Politics of Reproduction*. Albany: State University of New York Press, 2006.

Habermas, Jürgen. "A Conversation about God and the World." In *Religion and Rationality: Essays on Reason, God and Modernity*, edited by Eduardo Mendieta, 147–169. Oxford: Blackwell, 2000.

———. "Religion in the Public Sphere." *European Journal of Philosophy* 14, no. 4 (2006): 1–25.

Habermas, Jürgen, and Jacques Derrida. *Philosophy in a Time of Terror: Dialogues with Jürgen Habermas and Jacques Derrida*. Edited by Giovanna Borradori. Chicago: University of Chicago Press, 2003.

Habermas, Jürgen, and Joseph Ratzinger. *The Dialectics of Secularization*. San Francisco: Ignatius Press, 2006.

Heaney, Seamus. *The Redress of Poetry*. New York: Farrar, Straus and Giroux, 2011.

Hénaff, Marcel. *The Philosophers' Gift: Reexamining Reciprocity*. New York: Fordham University Press, 2019.

Higgins, Michael D. "Reflection on the Gorta Mór: The Great Irish Famine." In *When Ideas Matter: Speeches for an Ethical Republic*, 54–74. London: Zeus Head, 2016.

Huntington, Samuel. *The Clash of Civilizations and the Remaking of the World Order*. New York: Simon & Schuster, 2003.

———. *Who Are We? The Challenge to America's National Identity*. New York: Simon & Schuster, 2004.

Hyde, Lewis. *The Gift: Creativity and the Artist in the Modern World*. New York: Vintage Books, 1979.
Joyce, James. *Finnegans Wake*. New York: Viking Press, 1939.
Judt, Tony. *Postwar*. New York: Penguin, 2005.
Kant, Immanuel. *Critique of Pure Reason*. Translated and edited by Paul Guyer and Allen W. Wood. Cambridge: Cambridge University Press, 1998.
———. *Lectures on Ethics*. Translated by Louis Infield. New York: Harper & Row, 1963.
———. *Practical Philosophy*. Translated and edited by Mary J. Gregor. Cambridge: Cambridge University Press, 1996.
Katz, Claire Elise. *Levinas and the Crisis of Humanism*. Bloomington: Indiana University Press, 2013.
———. "Teaching Our Children Well: Pedagogy, Religion and the Future of Philosophy." *Crosscurrents* (Winter 2004): 530–545.
Kearney, Anne Bernard. *Lovers, Queens and Strangers*. Dublin: A and A Farmer, 1999.
Kearney, Richard. *Anatheism*. New York: Columbia University Press, 2010.
———. *Debates in Continental Philosophy: Conversations with Contemporary Thinkers*. New York: Fordham University Press, 2004.
———. "Double Hospitality—Between Word and Touch." *Journal for Continental Philosophy of Religion* 1 (2019): 71–89.
———. "Ecrire la chair: L'expression diacritique chez Merleau-Ponty." *Chiasmi International* 15 (Fall 2013): 183–198.
———. "Hermeneutics of Wounds." In *Unconscious Incarnations*, edited by Brian Becker et al., 21–42. New York: Routledge, 2018.
———. "Hospitality: Possible or Impossible." *Hospitality and Society* 5, nos. 2–3 (2013): 173–184.
———. "Linguistic Hospitality—The Risk of Translation." *Research in Phenomenology* 49 (2019): 1–8.
———. "Memory and Forgetting in Irish Culture." In *Recovering Memory: Irish Representations of Past and Present*, edited by Hedda Friberg, Irene Gilsenan, Nordin, and Lene Yding Pedersen, 2–19. Cambridge: Cambridge Scholars Publishing, 2007.
———. "Memory in Irish Culture." In *Memory Ireland*, edited by Oona Frawley, 3:138–151. Syracuse, NY: Syracuse University Press, 2014.
———. "Narrative Imagination: Between Ethics and Poetics." *Philosophy and Social Critique* 21, nos. 5–6 (1995): 173–190.
———. *Navigations: Collected Irish Essays, 1976–2006*. Syracuse, NY: Syracuse University Press, 2006.
———. *Postnationalist Ireland*. New York: Routledge, 1997.
———. *Strangers, Gods, and Monsters*. New York: Routledge, 2003.
———. *Touch: Recovering Our Most Vital Sense*. New York: Columbia University Press, 2021.

Kearney, Richard, ed. *Visions of Europe: Conversations on the Legacy and Future of Europe*. Dublin: Wolfhound Press/RTE, 1992.
Kearney, Richard, and Brian Treanor, eds. *Carnal Hermeneutics*. New York: Fordham University Press, 2015.
Kearney, Richard, and Mark Dooley, eds. *Questioning Ethics: Contemporary Debates in Philosophy*. New York: Routledge, 1999.
Kearney, Richard, and Sheila Gallagher. *Twinsome Minds: An Act of Double Remembrance*. Cork: Cork University Press, 2017.
Kearney, Richard, and Eileen Rizo-Patron, eds. *Traversing the Heart: Journeys of the Inter-Religious Imagination*. Leiden: Brill, 2010.
Kearney, Richard, and Kascha Semonovitch, eds. *Phenomenologies of the Stranger*. New York: Fordham University Press, 2011.
Kearney, Richard, and James Taylor, eds. *Hosting the Stranger: Between Religions*. New York: Continuum, 2011.
Keller, Catherine. *Cloud of the Impossible: Negative Theology and Planetary Entanglement*. New York: Columbia University Press, 2014.
———. *Intercarnations*. New York: Fordham University Press, 2017.
———. *Political Theology of the Earth*. New York: Columbia University Press, 2018.
Kiberd, Declan. *Inventing Ireland*. London: Vintage Books, 1996.
Kierkegaard, Søren. *The Sickness Unto Death*. Edited and translated by Howard V. Hong and Edna H. Hong. Princeton: Princeton University Press, 1980.
Korsgaard, Christine. "The Reasons We Can Share: An Attack on the Distinction Between Agent-Relative and Agent-Neutral Values." *Social Philosophy and Policy* 10, no. 1 (1993): 24–51.
———. *The Sources of Normativity*. Cambridge: Cambridge University Press, 1996.
Kristeva, Julia. "L'humanité redécouvre la solitude existentielle, le sens des limites et la mortalité." *Corriere del Sera*, March 29, 2020.
———. *Strangers to Ourselves*. New York: Columbia University Press, 1991.
Krog, Antjie. *Country of My Skull: Guilt, Sorrow, and the Limits of Forgiveness in the New South Africa*. New York: Broadway Books, 2000.
Levinas, Emmanuel. *Collected Philosophical Papers of Emmanuel Levinas*. Translated by Alphonso Lingis. The Hague: Martinus Nijhoff, 1987.
———. *Difficult Freedom: Essays on Judaism*. Translated by Seán Hand. Baltimore: Johns Hopkins University Press, 1990.
———. *Otherwise Than Being or Beyond Essence*. Translated by Alphonso Lingis. Pittsburgh: Duquesne University Press, 2011.
———. *Totality and Infinity: An Essay on Exteriority*. Translated by Alphonso Lingis. Pittsburgh: Duquesne University Press, 1969.
Lomax, Eric. *The Railway Man: A POW's Searing Account of War, Brutality, and Forgiveness*. New York: Norton, 1995.
Louv, Richard. *Our Wild Calling: How Connecting with Animals Can Transform Our Lives—and Save Theirs*. Chapel Hill, NC: Algonquin Books, 2019.

Lydenberg, Robin. "From Icon to Index: Some Contemporary Visions of the Irish Stone Cottage." In *Eire/land*, edited by Vera Kreilkamp, 127–133. Boston: McMullen Museum of Art, Boston College, 2003.

Macintyre, Alasdair. *After Virtue: A Study in Moral Theory*. Notre Dame, IN: University of Notre Dame Press, 2007.

Manoussakis, John. "Coronations: Notes from the Quarantine." *The New Polis*, April 10, 2020.

Mauss, Marcel. *The Gift*. New York: Routledge, 1990.

Meaney, Thomas. "Who's Your Dance Partner? Europe Inside Africa." *London Review of Books* 41, no. 21 (November 9, 2019).

Mensch, James. *Levinas's Existential Analytic: A Commentary on Totality and Infinity*. Evanston, IL: Northwestern University Press, 2015.

Monge, Claudio. *Dieu hôte: Recherche historique et théologique sur les rituels de l'hospitalité*. Paris: Zeta Books, 2008.

Moyaert, Marianne. "The (Un-)Translatability of Religions? Ricoeur's Linguistic Hospitality as Model for Interreligious Dialogue in Exchange." *Journal of Missiological and Ecumenical Research* 37 (2008): 337–364.

Moyaert, Marianne, and Joris Geldhof. *Ritual Participation and Interreligious Dialogue: Boundaries, Transgressions and Innovations*. London: Bloomsbury, 2016.

Nancy, Jean-Luc. *Noli Me Tangere: On the Raising of the Body*. Translated by Sarah Clift. New York: Fordham University Press, 2008.

Nussbaum, Martha. *For Love of Country*. Boston: Beacon, 2002.

Prichard, H. A. "Does Moral Philosophy Rest on a Mistake?" *Mind* 21 (1912): 21–37.

Reath, Andrews. *Agency and Autonomy in Kant's Moral Theory*. Oxford: Oxford University Press, 2006.

Reath, Andrews, and Jens Timmerman, eds. *Kant's Critique of Practical Reason: A Critical Guide*. Cambridge: Cambridge University Press, 2010.

Ricoeur, Paul. "Entretien Hans Küng-Paul Ricoeur: Les religions, la violence et la paix. Pour une Ethique Planétaire, Arte. 5 April 1996." *Sens* 5 (1998): 211–230.

———. *La memoire, l'histoire, l'oubli*. Paris: Éditions du Seuil, 2000.

———. "Life in Quest of Narrative." In *On Paul Ricoeur: Narrative and Interpretation*, edited by David Wood, 20–33. London: Routledge, 1991.

———. *Memory, History and Forgetting*. Translated by David Pellauer. Chicago: University of Chicago Press, 2005.

———. *Oneself as Another*. Translated by Kathleen Blamey. Chicago: University of Chicago Press, 1992.

———. *On Translation*. Translated by Eileen Brennan. London: Routledge, 2006.

———. *Paul Ricoeur: The Hermeneutics of Action*. Edited by Richard Kearney. London: Sage, 1996.

———. "Reflections on a New Ethos for Europe." *Philosophy & Social Criticism* 21, nos. 5–6 (1995): 3–13.

———. *Time and Narrative, Volume 3*. Translated by Kathleen Blamey and David Pellauer. Chicago: University of Chicago Press, 1990.

Rohr, Richard. "Making Do with More: Economy Old and New." In Daily Meditations, Center for Action and Contemplation. November 25, 2019, cac.org/making-do-with-more-2019-11-25.

———. "Moral Capitalism." In Daily Meditations, Center for Action and Contemplation. November 27, 2019, cac.org/moral-capitalism-2019-11-27.

Sandel, Michael. "Are We All in This Together?" *New York Times*, April 13, 2020.

Scheler, Max. *The Nature of Sympathy*. London: Taylor & Francis, 2017.

Schott, Robin May. "Kant and Arendt on Hospitality." *Jahrbuch für Recht und Ethik/Annual Review of Law and Ethics* 17 (2009): 183–194.

Sen, Amartya. *Identity and Violence*. New York: Norton, 2007.

Simon, Arthur. *How Much Is Enough? Hungering for God in an Affluent Culture*. Grand Rapids, MI: Baker Books, 2003.

Speight, Allen. "Arendt on Narrative Theory and Practice." *College Literature* 38, no. 1 (Winter 2011): 115–130.

Stein, Edith. *On the Problem of Empathy*. Edited and translated by Waltraut Stein. Washington, DC: ICS Publishers, 1989.

Steinbock, Anthony. *Phenomenology and Mysticism*. Bloomington: Indiana University Press, 2007.

Strahn, Anna. *Levinas, Subjectivity, Education: Towards an Ethics of Radical Responsibility*. Hoboken, NJ: Wiley Blackwell, 2012.

Taylor, Charles. *A Secular Age*. Cambridge, MA: Harvard University Press, 2007.

Taylor, Paul. "The Ethics of Respect for Nature." *Environmental Ethics* 3, no. 3 (1981): 197–218.

Teenan, Tim. "Coronavirus Has Killed the Power of Touch. How Do We Reconnect?" *Daily Beast*, April 16, 2020.

Twist, Lynn, and Teresa Barker. *The Soul of Money: Transforming Your Relationship with Money and Life*. New York: Norton, 2017.

Veldsman, Daniël, and Yolande Steenkamp, eds. *Debating Otherness with Richard Kearney: Perspectives from South Africa*. Durbanville: Aosis Publishing, 2018.

Vila-Chã, João J. Miranda, ed. O Dom, a Verdade, e a Morte: Abordagens e Perspectivas/The Gift, Truth, and Death: Approaches and Perspectives. Special edition of *Revista Portuguesa de Filosofia* 65 (2009).

Wares, Owen. "Kant on Moral Sensibility and Moral Motivation." *Journal of the History of Philosophy* 52, no. 4 (October 2014): 727–746.

Wiedmer, Caroline. *The Claims of Memory: Representations of the Holocaust in Contemporary Germany and France*. Ithaca, NY: Cornell University Press, 1999.

Index

Adorno, Theodor 120n17
Al-Assad, Bashar 54
Alexander, Laura 119n11, 134n6
Anderson, Benedict 31
Arafat, Yasser 50
Arendt, Hannah 11, 13, 23, 75–76, 84–92, 94, 101, 127n22, 129n2, 130n7, 132–33n15, 18–21, 23, 26
Aristotle 33, 50, 56–57, 88, 92–96, 120n17
Augustine, Saint 48, 51
Averroes 48
Avicenna 48

Becker, Brian 120n17
Balch, Alex 114n9
Balfour, Lindsay 9–10, 12, 116nn18,20
Baring, Edward 115n13
Barker, Teresa 115n15
Benhabib, Seyla 133n15
Benjamin, Walter 46–47, 65, 69, 126nn19–21
Benveniste, Emile 20, 118n4
Bergdahl, Lovisa 47, 124n6, 125n17, 126n19
Bergo, Bettina 79
Berman, Antoine 20, 118n5

Bernard Kearney, Anne 129n28
Bhaba, Homi 125n8
Bin Laden, Osama 44
Blanco, Richard 10, 11
Block, Peter 115n14
Borradori, Giovanna 124n6
Bougas, Angelos 119n11
Boursier, Helen 102–3, 119n11, 134n6
Brandt, Willy 41
Brewer, Talbot 13, 88–95, 133nn1–4, 134n5
Brueggemann, Walter 115n14
Buber, Martin 20
Bulley, Dan 114n9
Bush, George 44
Butler, James 27
Butler, Judith 80, 83, 131n8, 132n14

Callaghan, Eoin 31
Caputo, John 4, 6, 115n12, 118n8
Carson, Anne 26
Casanova 54
Casey, Edward 9 116n19
Cavanaugh-O'Keefe, John 113n3
Celan, Paul 120n17
Chamberlain, Neville 54
Chomsky, Noam 26

145

Cicura, Donatien 125n8
Cohn-Bendit, Daniel 40
Connolly, James 34
Cornille, Catherine 126n20
Corpt, Elizabeth 120n17

Dausner, René 5–7, 102, 114n9, 115nn10,13, 132n13
Davis, Bret 104n3
De Klerk, F. W. 50
De Kock, Eugene 51–53
De Vries, Hent 124n6
Denizet-Lewis, Benoit 134n1
Derrida, Jacques 3–6, 12–13, 21–23, 26, 44–47, 56, 64–65, 69–70, 78, 82, 114nn5,7, 115nn12–13, 118nn7–8, 119n7, 123n30, 124–25nn6, 9,11, 126nn18,20, 132n13
Dooley, Mark 115n12, 119n12, 120n14, 126n20
Dufourmantelle, Anne 3

Eisenstein, Charles 116n15
Egoyan, Atom 120n17
Eliot, T. S. 53
Ellsworth, Elizabeth Ann 121n19
Emmanuel, Steven 114n3
Epstein, Tom 118n6

FitzGerald, Gearóid Mór 27
Flyntz, Kristin 105
Foster, Roy 37, 121n22
Frawley, Oona 120n14
Freud, Sigmund 33, 54, 119n12, 122n24
Friberg, Hedda 126n1
Friel, Brian 31, 34
Fukuyama, Francis 125n8

Gadamer, Hans-Georg 40, 92, 123n32
Gallagher, Sheila 29, 31, 119n14, 120n17
Gandhi, Mahatma 50
Geldhof, Joris 124n5
Gibbons, Luke 37, 121n22
Gilsenan Nordin, Irene 126n1
Giuliani, Rudy 121n23
Gobodo-Madikizela, Pumla 50–53, 126n5, 127nn6,10,13,18,20–22

Goodman, David 121n17
Gordon, Peter 115n13
Griffith, Arthur 34

Habermas, Jürgen 12, 44–8, 78, 124n36, 124–25nn6,9–12,15,17, 126n19
Havel, Vaclav 41
Haweed, Urwa 127n25, 128n28
Heaney, Seamus 30, 119n13
Hegel, G. W. F. 6, 70
Hénaff, Marcel 4–5, 114n8
Henry, Paul 47
Higgins, Michael D. 120n14
Hillesum, Etty 41, 120n17
Hitler, Adolf 44, 54
Hobbes, Thomas 65
Homer 19, 49
Hong, Edward and Edna 130n6
Horatio 47
Howe, Fanny 55
Hume, John 41
Huntington, Samuel 44, 135n8
Husserl, Edmund 21, 50, 126n20
Hwang, Alexander 119n11, 134n6
Hyde, Lewis 114n6

Infield, Louis 130n9
Irving, George and William 31

Jinping, Xi 54
Johnson, Boris 2
Jones, Jim 54
Jong-un, Kim 45
Joyce, James 20, 30, 34, 120n16
Judt, Tony 121n19
Jung, Carl 54

Kang, Tian 127n15, 128n27
Kant, Immanuel 1–2, 5–6, 13, 61–79, 81–85, 87–89, 91, 94, 96, 103, 129nn2–5, 130nn7–9, 131nn6,11, 132nn12–13, 133n21
Katz, Claire 134n4
Keller, Catherine 116n17
Kiberd, Declan 37, 121n22
Kierkegaard, Søren 54, 69–70, 129n6, 130n9; Anti-Climacus 129n6; Johannes de Silencio 6

King Jr., Martin Luther 64, 117n23
Kinsella, Thomas 30
Koresh, David 54
Koslowski, P. 119n7
Kreilkamp, Vera 122n25
Kristeva, Julia 3, 21, 50, 118n6, 121n21, 126n22, 136n4
Krog, Antjie 120n17, 127n23

Lanzmann, Claude 120n17
Levi, Primo 120n17
Levinas, Emmanuel 3, 7, 13, 22–23, 26, 47, 75–85, 88–89, 91, 94–95, 103, 114n5, 119n7, 130nn1,3, 131nn4–7,10, 132n12, 134n4
Lin, Maya 39
Lingis, Alphonso 131n10
Lomax, Eric 127n17
Louv, Richard, 116–17n23
Luther, Martin 20
Lyndenberg, Robin 122n25, 123n27, 28

MacIntyre, Alasdair 89, 94–95
Maimonides 20, 48
Malinowski, Bronislaw 4
Mandela, Nelson 50
Manoussakis, John 136n2, 121n17
Manson, Charlie 54
Marion, Jean-Luc 4, 118n8
Mauss, Marcel 4, 114n6
McGuinness, Martin 50
McKnight, John 115n14
Meaney, Thomas 2, 113n1
Mensch, James 130n1
Merleau-Ponty, Maurice 50, 56
Michelangelo 127–28n26
Milena 120n17
Monge, Claudio 124n2
Mountbatten, Louis 50
Moyaert, Marianne 124n5, 127n25
Murphy, Tom 123n29

Nancy, Jean-Luc 128n26
Nussbaum, Martha 125n8

O'Connor, James 37
O'Faolain, Séan 30
O'Flaherty, Tomas 123n29

Paisley, Ian 50
Pataki, George 121n23
Paul, Saint 20
Pearse, Patrick 34
Pellauer, David 123n30
Pétain, Phillipe, 54
Plato 125n8
Proust, Marcel 20
Putin, Vladimir 54

Oz, Amos 120n17

Rabin, Yitzhak 50
Ratzinger, Joseph 44, 46
Reed-Sandoval, Amy 98, 134n2
Reich, Wilhelm 54
Ricoeur, Paul 3, 4, 6, 12–13, 17–19, 21–22, 24–26, 33, 35, 39–41, 43–44, 56, 66, 86, 92, 113n3, 114nn3,5, 117–18nn1–2, 118n9, 118n1, 119nn7,12, 121nn18,20, 123nn30–31, 33, 124nn1,5, 126n5, 127n9, 132n13, 133n24
Rizo-Patron, Eileen 118n6
Rohr, Richard 7–8, 115n14, 116nn15–16
Rumi 48

Sadat, Anwar 41
Sahtouris, Elisabet 116n17
Sandel, Michael 106, 136n3
Scanlon, Michael 188n8
Scheler, Max 126n20
Schott, Robin May 63, 74, 86, 129n2, 130n10, 132n15, 133n21
Semonovitch, Kascha 14, 118n6, 127n19
Sen, Amartya 125n8
Shakespeare, William 19, 37
Sheehan, Ronan 119n9
Shizuteru, Ueda 114n3
Simon, Arthur 8, 116n16
Socrates 86, 98
Speight, Allen 133n24
Spiegelman, Art 120n17
Spielberg, Steven 120n17
Stalin, Joseph 44, 54
Steenkamp, Yolande 119n7, 126n5
Stein, Edith 126n20
Stevens, Cyril and William 31

Sullivan, L. E. 124n6
Sweeney, Maurice 119n8

Taylor, James 14, 113n3, 118nn3,6, 136n5
Teenan, Tim 136n1
Thomas, Saint 48
Tippett, Krista 10, 116n21, 136n4
Tolle, Brian 35–39, 121–22nn23,25, 123n28
Treanor, Brian 127n19, 131n7
Trump, Donald 2, 5, 10, 44, 54
Tutu, Desmond 53
Twist, Lynn 115n15

Veldsman, Daniël 119n7, 126n5
Venetis, Clay 119n11
Vila-Chã, João J. Miranda 114n6
Virgil 20
Von Ribbentrop, Joachim 54
Vosloo, Robert 126n5

Wares, Owen 129n5
Warner, Marina 2, 49, 113n2, 126n2
Weil, Simone 3

Yates, Chris 118n6
Yding Pedersen, Lene 126n1
Yeats, W. B. 30, 32

Richard Kearney is Charles Seelig Chair of Philosophy at Boston College and author and editor of more than forty books on contemporary philosophy and culture. He is founding editor of the Guestbook Project and has been engaged in developing a postnationalist philosophy of peace and empathy over several decades. His most relevant books on this subject include *Strangers, Gods and Monsters* (2001), *Postnationalist Ireland (*1998), *Hosting the Stranger* (2012), *Phenomenologies of the Stranger* (2010), *Imagination Now* (2019), and *Touch: Recovering Our Most Vital Sense* (2021).

Melissa Fitzpatrick is an Assistant Professor of the Practice in Ethics for the Portico Program in Boston College's Carroll School of Management and the Director of Pedagogy for Guestbook Project. Her research focuses on the intersection between contemporary virtue ethics and post-Kantian continental philosophy. She has also done integrated teaching, research, and community outreach in pre-college philosophy in the Mississippi Delta and on the Mexican–American border in El Paso, Texas.

Perspectives in Continental Philosophy
John D. Caputo, series editor

Recent titles:

Kirill Chepurin and Alex Dubilet, eds., *Nothing Absolute: German Idealism and the Question of Political Theology*

John D. Caputo, *In Search of Radical Theology: Expositions, Explorations, Exhortations*

Galen A. Johnson, Mauro Carbone, and Emmanuel de Saint Aubert, *Merleau-Ponty's Poetics: Figurations of Literature and Philosophy*

Ole Jakob Løland, *Pauline Ugliness: Jacob Taubes and the Turn to Paul.*

Marika Rose, *A Theology of Failure: <hac>Zi<hac>zek against Christian Innocence.*

Marc Crépon, *Murderous Consent: On the Accommodation of Violent Death.* Translated by Michael Loriaux and Jacob Levi, Foreword by James Martel

Emmanuel Falque, *The Guide to Gethsemane: Anxiety, Suffering, and Death.* Translated by George Hughes.

Emmanuel Alloa, *Resistance of the Sensible World: An Introduction to Merleau-Ponty.* Translated by Jane Marie Todd. Foreword by Renaud Barbaras.

Françoise Dastur, *Questions of Phenomenology: Language, Alterity, Temporality, Finitude.* Translated by Robert Vallier.

Jean-Luc Marion, *Believing in Order to See: On the Rationality of Revelation and the Irrationality of Some Believers.* Translated by Christina M. Gschwandtner.

Adam Y. Wells, ed., *Phenomenologies of Scripture.*

An Yountae, *The Decolonial Abyss: Mysticism and Cosmopolitics from the Ruins.*

Jean Wahl, *Transcendence and the Concrete: Selected Writings.* Edited and with an Introduction by Alan D. Schrift and Ian Alexander Moore.

Colby Dickinson, *Words Fail: Theology, Poetry, and the Challenge of Representation.*

Emmanuel Falque, *The Wedding Feast of the Lamb: Eros, the Body, and the Eucharist.* Translated by George Hughes.

Emmanuel Falque, *Crossing the Rubicon: The Borderlands of Philosophy and Theology.* Translated by Reuben Shank. Introduction by Matthew Farley.

Colby Dickinson and Stéphane Symons (eds.), *Walter Benjamin and Theology.*

Don Ihde, *Husserl's Missing Technologies.*

William S. Allen, *Aesthetics of Negativity: Blanchot, Adorno, and Autonomy.*

Jeremy Biles and Kent L. Brintnall, eds., *Georges Bataille and the Study of Religion.*

Tarek R. Dika and W. Chris Hackett, *Quiet Powers of the Possible: Interviews in Contemporary French Phenomenology.* Foreword by Richard Kearney.

Richard Kearney and Brian Treanor, eds., *Carnal Hermeneutics.*

A complete list of titles is available at http://fordhampress.com.

www.ingramcontent.com/pod-product-compliance
Lightning Source LLC
Chambersburg PA
CBHW030443300426
44112CB00009B/1144